E FOR KEN

…eth Steven has a ready sensitivity to the beauty of
moments.' *THE HERALD*

…re is a grave beauty in these lines, revealing a poetic
…e of great sensitivity.' ALEXANDER MCCALL SMITH

…eth has a rare gift of being able to transmute the mun-
…nto the mesmerizing, in a kind of poetic alchemy.'
…RYMAN

…is poetry of rare honesty, touching on the vital needs
…spirit in our age and manifesting a profound aware-
…and concern for the world about us. JOHN F DEANE

'F… …talent for capturing the startling, original image …
… …fine, fine poet' *NEW SHETLANDER*

Beneath the Ice

In search of the Sami

Kenneth Steven

with photographs by
Kristina Hayward

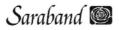

Saraband

Published by Saraband
Suite 202, 98 Woodlands Road
Glasgow, G3 6HB, Scotland
www.saraband.net

ISBN: 9781910192276
ebook: 9781910192283

Printed in the EU on sustainably sourced paper.

Contents

*For Lars, Biret
and John Cesar –*

the best of friends

Introduction

IT WAS THE WRITER CS LEWIS who spoke about having been born with a sense of northern-ness. The idea of that certainly resonates with me, but perhaps I just grew into a northern skin; it's hard now to know which is true. But from my earliest days it was forests, wolves and snow that formed the backdrop to a mythic landscape; I even caught it in the music of certain composers whose work I heard, however young I must have been.

To describe it as a calling almost certainly sounds over-romantic and cloying, yet that's how I would express it, all the same. I devoured writing that sought to capture the essence of this northern spirit, and as a result the first books that I read were works of high fantasy that built on a Nordic landscape.

Years later, when I first took Nordlandsbanen, the ten hours of railway journey from Trondheim to Bodø, north of the Arctic Circle, I felt that I had achieved it at last. I was all but flying north and ever further north through forest and over tundra to a landscape I felt embedded in my soul. I was as excited as a five-year-old. In a strange and inexplicable way, I was going home at last.

It counted for a great deal that my parents were lovers of this landscape too. The Nordic world had influenced them both; my father was stationed in Iceland during the Second World War and returned to Scotland destined to be a devotee of Iceland's mountains, glaciers and lakes for the rest of his days. My mother, bizarrely enough, learned Norwegian when living in Canada. My father and mother were united by hills and mountains; they were both passionate climbers, and it was the peaks of Iceland and Norway that almost certainly made up their yearning for north. It was embedded in my sister too; she led the first women's climbing expedition from Scotland to Greenland – the party not only climbed there, they named "new" peaks too.

So I do see that the likelihood of my becoming fascinated by a Mediterranean or North African landscape was hardly great. I grew up in a house surrounded by books on Alpine and Nordic expeditions and adventures, many of which I leafed through too. But it was never the mountains that tugged at me; after being dragged up too many Scottish Munros the aversion therapy worked once and for all. I wasn't interested in the mountains of the north; it was the north in and of itself I wanted. In fact my first year in Norway was to be spent in Vestlandet, the fjord country north of Bergen – with the kind of mountain-scape around me the rest of my family would have given their eye teeth to experience. I was always drawn to the true north, beyond the Arctic Circle, where paradoxically enough the mountains became not unlike the hills of home – long stretched wolves with moorlands in front of them covered in scrub birch and heather.

Before I went to Norway for the first time, I had already learned of the Sami (except that back then they would have been called the Lapps). I can remember standing in front of

4

our television set, moved by these black and white images of Sami in their traditional blue, red and gold costumes – chained to machinery, which I later realised was part of their protest against the building of a dam in a part of Norway immensely important to the Sami. I'm not sure how much I understood; I'm wary of pouring too much adult awareness now into what I must have been at ten or eleven. All I do know is that I was moved and I was fascinated. I wanted to understand more, that was for certain. I knew at least that these people were protesting, that it was their northern territory that was under some kind of threat.

I felt the same kind of melding of fascination and yearning to understand more when I encountered a tiny fragment of the Sami world for the first time a year or two later. My parents took me to Sweden and then Norway; they drove up to the heart of the fjord country and took the Bergen ferry back to Newcastle. At some point during our time in Norway we came across what was then called a Lapp camp. They may well have been Sami from central Norway, their camp established to sell carved knives and reindeer horn trinkets to tourists. I can vividly remember running up onto the hillside to meet them; I was hungry to understand their world, to talk to them. But talking was the one thing we couldn't do; their languages would have been Sami and Norwegian – if they did know some English then it's more than likely it would have been limited. So I met them and remembered well enough the images I had seen on our little black and white television set not long before. I wanted to ask questions but I didn't know how, and all I could do was exchange a hundred-kroner note for a set of reindeer antlers I brought home uselessly to

Scotland. I was no further on, but my eagerness to find out was stronger than ever.

Landscape and people were bound up together: the Sami inhabited this mythic landscape that was so deeply embedded in my psyche. I still knew next to nothing about them except that they herded reindeer, but that northern-ness formed an umbilical, allowed me to understand something inexpressible at a level deeper than words. I now wanted to *find* the words to know both them and their landscape.

* * *

All through secondary school days I longed for Norway, wanted to find some way of returning after the long and miserable years at school were finally over. But staying for any length of time in Norway back in the 1980s was more or less impossible: a residence permit was absolutely necessary, and getting one verged on the impossible. The only real glimmer of possibility lay in study of some kind, but beyond that it was nothing less than guesswork. The one person I thought could help me was Howard Liddell, an architect living in our part of Highland Perthshire, and every year he went over to lecture at the Oslo Summer School. I begged Howard to do some sleuthing on my behalf; to seek out anything he could find that might build me a boat, almost literally, to get me back to Norway.

Howard returned with a brochure for the Folk High Schools. At that point the concept meant nothing to me, and bear in mind that this was long before the dawn of the Internet. It transpired there were Folk High Schools all across Scandinavia. Some 200 years ago a Danish priest came up with the idea; I'm not sure if originally the whole sense of a gap year was there, but that's effectively what it has become. Most students will have just finished secondary school; most will never have lived away from home before, and they are at the perfect stage for a year of discovery and adventure in an entirely new place.

The majority of Folk High Schools are to be found in the countryside. It's not just about a nice location: the natural world and a greater understanding of it lies at the heart of the whole ethos of Folk High School. Every school offers different subjects; some will have teachers of philosophy or Spanish, but the emphasis is often on practical skills such as woodworking and boatbuilding. This business of the outdoors matters a great deal: there will be weekends away for the whole school – staff and students alike – for building snow holes and skiing, or being in cabins without electricity. It's about learning to live in community – to work together and get on together.

Let me give an example of how Folk High School might change a young person's life. A seventeen-year-old arrives from Bergen for the start of the school year with little more than his electric guitar. He's thrilled that he's found a place at a school that has a special guitar course: it's the only thing in his head. The teacher works with him and the others in the group for a few weeks then tells them that there's a cluster of younger children in the local community who would love to learn to play the guitar but their teacher has moved away. Would one of the group be willing to meet them and pass on some skills?

The boy from Bergen says yes. All winter and the spring that follows he works with the little group in the village, and at the end of the school year they put on a concert at the Folk High School. Everyone's life is changed.

Back then I was aware of none of this. All I did know was that I wanted to get to one of these colleges, that this was the best way – if not the only way – for me to find a residence permit for a year's stay in Norway. But the Folk High School year is far from free, and scholarships few and far between. Every year the Norwegian government offers a handful to youngsters from abroad, in thanks for the assistance Norway was given during the dark years of the Second World War. I now did all I could to secure one of these free places – and was fortunate enough to be successful.

I returned from that first year in Norway feeling a new person. In truth I didn't want to come back at all; I had fallen head over heels in love with this country and everything it was made of. In my late teens I was still young enough to soak up a new language like a sponge; by the end of that academic year in Vestlandet I was speaking far more Norwegian than English, and I had a wide circle of friends – more by far than I had left behind in Scotland.

But back in the 1980s, as I have said, you had to have a residence permit to stay in Norway, and obtaining one was anything but easy. The police came to the Folk High School where I had been studying; they visited the college the day before my visa was due to expire. They were very friendly, but they wanted to be sure all the same that I knew I was going home the next day.

I went to Glasgow University with nothing less than lead in my heart. The grimness of the city that first autumn only served to reinforce my miserable missing of Norway.

Every night before I went to sleep I used to play *Solveigs Sang* by Grieg. In some ways I survived that lonely first year of university by promising myself that after all this was done I would return to Norway, and that now I would find the true north. That goal sustained me and remained with me, long after I had found good friends in the city and had ceased to be quite as miserable as I had at the beginning.

During that first year in the west of Norway I had spent long hours talking to one teacher in particular. He heaped coals on the fire of my yearning for the far north. Fritz had grown up in Tromsø, way north of the Arctic Circle, and he told me wonderful stories of the northern wildscape, encouraged me to get there if I possibly could.

In the years that followed, Chernobyl happened. I was well aware of the radioactive cloud that had hung over Arctic Scandinavia as an unnaturally heavy rain descended. I was conscious of the damage to the tundra; saw footage of reindeer being taken for slaughter because the mosses they grazed on were saturated with radioactive poisons. But this only added to my determination to go still further north and find out what had happened to the people, to discover if anything at all of their way of life had survived. I worked on with my degree in Glasgow, but I set my sights on a return to Norway, and this time to the far north.

* * *

It was still necessary to have a residence permit to stay for any length of time in Norway, so simply travelling over to explore was an impossibility. But I had loved my year at Folk High School in Vestlandet, and now I found a place at another of these colleges – this time not far from the town of Bodø, a hundred miles north of the Circle. Here I could study *friluftsliv* (literally, outdoor life) and be employed as a student counsellor, thus having my fees paid. Here at last I found the Sami world I had longed for, and the chance to ask the questions I had carried for so many years.

I was living not far from the Sami coastal settlement of Tysfjord (pronounced "Toos-fjord"). There were several students from Tysfjord attending my college, and I fear I must have bombarded them with questions the moment I first realised what their background was. They were naturally enough more than a little wary of my over-enthusiasm, and I well remember the times they told me tall stories, only to hoot with laughter afterwards because in my naivety I had believed them implicitly. If I learned nothing else early on, it was that with the Sami there could be a form of merriment not far beneath the surface all the time; a playing of games and a delight in practical jokes that couldn't be supressed. In fact, the more traps I fell into with their stories, the more they delighted in the game. But I still hadn't found anyone to speak to from the northern Sami community, and I was still hundreds of miles south of their world.

What I did instead was to work hard with my study of that world. I was fluent in Norwegian and devoured all the books I could find from the local library on the Sami story. Books were sent to me from Karasjok and Kautokeino, two of the principal Sami settlements in central Finnmark. If anything I worked harder at all this than ever I had done in my trudging years of study at Glasgow University. But now I *wanted* to learn and I had a chance to learn. I began to understand something of Sami history, religion, culture; more than anything I started to realise the centuries of discrimination and sheer struggle. I probably read for the first time about the fight for Alta, the demonstration I had caught a tiny glimpse of all those years before on television in Scotland.

It was only at the college year's close that it happened, that first encounter with the northern Sami world. There was to be a conference for Folk High Schools right up on the then Soviet border at a place called Svanvik, and I was invited to attend. Part of the visit was to include a trip to the town of Nikel on the Soviet side, and because of all the stringent security requirements, passports had to be handed in for the processing of red tape (what an apt phrase) several months in advance.

I can't honestly remember now why I never went with the main group to Nikel in the end. All I do know is that I ended up staying behind at the Folk High School in Svanvik feeling that life was most unfair. Here had been a unique opportunity to experience something of Soviet existence far north of the Arctic Circle and I was missing out. At some point I must have been told that a bus trip was being arranged for all those who hadn't had the chance to go to Nikel. I remember getting onto that bus, and noticing at once there were only perhaps four or five others with me.

We duly drove to a place on the border and took pictures of each other sticking our hands out over the fence, for here it was little more than a metal structure separating one bit of tundra from another. In due course we got back onto the bus, drove on, and stopped at a museum where

I found a book on some aspect or other of the Sami story and had to buy it. But I discovered I didn't have sufficient kroner in my pocket and decided I could do worse than ask one of the others in the group if he'd be kind enough to lend me the rest until we were back at the college. That was no problem and the missing kroner were supplied at once, but the man I had asked was intrigued by the book I'd chosen. It transpired he was the headmaster of the Sami Folk High School in Karasjok. I had no idea that such a place existed.

So we talked when we got back onto the bus; at least he must have talked and I babbled – about the whole story that led up to my coming to Arctic Norway to find the Sami. I talked too about the Highland world I had inherited from my mother: a Gaelic-speaking and devoutly religious community. It turned out that we both had half an inheritance: Lars had grown up almost as far south as possible in Norway, with a Sami father and a mother from near Oslo, while my mother was a Gael but my father was from Helensburgh – very much a Lowlander.

I remember the conversation continuing for perhaps four hours or more back at the Folk High School in Svanvik. It was the longest conversation I'd ever had in Norwegian. I remember leaving Lars' boarding house late that evening, half-drunk on all I had heard and learned. For the half of Lars that belonged to the Sami world was from Finnmark. He lived now with his wife in Karasjok, at the very heart of northern Sami country with reindeer herders on every side. He told me that I had to come and visit them: of course I must.

ONE

North

HAMMERFEST WAS NOTHING MORE than the stink of dead fish. A long huddle of bleach-white factory sheds, a few aimless streets and the stink of fish. Numberless handlebars of gulls steering low over greyness.

It did not help that I lay face downwards on a pavement, or that it was sleeting. It was midsummer morning and I was shivering like some thin, scabby dog. Behind me, the great gleaming crystal of the coastal steamer curved out towards open sea again and boomed twice, long and deep, heading towards the last Arctic ports on her itinerary

I had food poisoning. I was saved by a Danish doctor, who dragged me into his surgery and saw to the two ends of me that were leaking. At the same time he took my mind off the discomfort by talking. Danes are almost invariably amiable – the human equivalent of puppies – handicapped only by a language that their Norwegian cousins rudely describe as sounding like a throat disease. I wondered why on earth he had come to this jagged fossil dinosaur of a place to work; usually Danes are frightened of hills – after all, if you climb onto a house roof in Jutland you can more or less see the Houses of Parliament at the other end of the country.

He had wanted to get away, he said. Well, he'd succeeded there. He'd dreamed of finding the north, the real north. All right, I understood that too. I was there for the same reason. But the illnesses were killing him, he said. What illnesses? Whisky and tobacco; everyone was dying of whisky and tobacco.

When I came out again into the raw aquamarine air of Hammerfest I wasn't altogether surprised. A solitary Norwegian, with a hangover from the Saturday night that had just become Sunday morning, was lolling against a high fence like a rag doll, singing. I shivered. I wondered if all this wasn't too much for humanity, a few degrees north of sanity, a place that was never meant to be.

But going inland, the landscape changed. The grey canine teeth of the mountains softened into dark breasts of hills, and trees started greening their slopes – tall, jade pines that hid little gems of water. I reached Karasjok in the evening, an evening that didn't get dark but only grew bluer.

Lars, who was the only Sami I had ever known, and the passport for my journey, greeted me like a brother. He had the dark almond eyes of a Mongolian hunter; thin, straight, dark hair. A Norwegian who wasn't a Norwegian, who would have been branded a drunk and a work-shy Lapp (spit) in every town between Tromsø and Tønsberg. Forty years ago. Maybe even now.

He and his wife, Biret, had a dishwasher, an electric carving knife, satellite television. "Are you surprised?" he laughed at me, and maybe I looked it. "Nomadic Lapplanders with all the right Western toys!" On the table in the living room I saw his traditional Sami costume, a reindeer horn hunting knife and birch drinking cup – and a mobile phone. All in one heap. That was the Sami world I was to keep attempting to sort out in my head time after time over the next days.

But it was *jonsok*, midsummer night, and there was a celebration to join. The back garden crackled and spat with a bonfire, and friends who had come with curiosity to meet the strange traveller murmured in Sami among the long blue shadows. There were fires all across Karasjok, into the hills that reached towards the Finnish border – amber fire-flies with midges around them, the clink of glasses, the echoes of *joik*.

*Joik*ing is the way the Sami celebrate their world. At birth every child is given their own *joik*, but the song will grow and change within each individual as he or she stretches towards adolescence and adulthood. When it is sung a last time at their graveside it will be complete, it will form the book of their life, the celebration of their being.

But that night the *joik* told of reindeer, of the ancient world of the Sami, of bears and wolves and the great journeys of the herders across the tundra, right to the edges of Russia:

Somewhere deep inside me
I hear
a voice calling
and hear the joik *of the blood*
deep
from life's boundary
to life's boundary.

All this is my home –
these fjords, rivers, lakes,
the frost, the sunlight, the storm,
the night and daytime of these moorlands –
joy and sorrow,
sister and brother.
All this is my home
*and I carry it in my heart.**

I dreamed that night of being among the bellies of blue whales. They were calling to each other across the oceans of the world and though only a few remained their song was made of the same sounds and was understood in the west, the north, the south and the east. I woke up in the morning listening to the thatch of birdsong in the birch trees, feeling clean and scoured as a single bone, washed up on a new and strange shore.

* * *

"I'm taking you somewhere," said Lars after breakfast. The morning sky was like a single pane of glass, full of the yellow resin of the pines. The traffic was already loud in the town streets: Germans with their Dormobiles, young Norwegians whose cars thudded with heavy metal, trucks on their way to Sweden, Finland and Russia. We took the road that wound down close to the river through avenues of birches whose leaves glinted like silver coins.

---

* An English translation of a Nils-Aslak Valkeapää *joik*, which appears in the original Sami in *Ruoktu Váimmus* (DAT, 1985).

Lars stopped the car by the church. "The only building in Karasjok that survived 1944," he said, getting out. "Everything else was burned by the retreating Germans. The Sami went back to the hills, abandoned their settled lives and existed as they always had. That whole winter. Come into the churchyard with me; I want to show you something – the story of the Sami."

We went to the far end of the graveyard, shrouded by older and darker trees. There was nothing – I saw nothing. The ground was covered in leaves and moss. I looked help-lessly at Lars as he stood beside me.

"This ground is full of Sami people – men, women and children. They didn't mark their graves in the days before Christianity, they didn't think of it. The people were part of the land, in life as in death."

We walked on, twenty feet, to the first row of neat white stones. "What do you notice now? What do you see on the graves?"

I looked. Arild Johansen, Gunhild Rasmussen, Ottar Brekke...

I looked at him. "Norwegian names?"

He nodded fiercely. "Yes, the whole lot. Not a Sami name among them. Why? Because Sami was illegal, because Sami names were illegal. It was the lowest time we ever knew. Our language was stopped in our throats, and if we were to achieve anything in Norway we had to become set-tled, we had to become mortgaged to a town. Even then we were still second-class citizens; dirty, untrustworthy oddities made fun of in the playground and in the parlia-ment in Oslo. Even the church made us look at ourselves with shame and seek repentance for what we were."

I went forward again along the wavering gravel path. I was walking though time. Again Lars ordered me to stop.

"This is my generation," he said. "Look very carefully at the names on the stones, the dates. Think about them. Tell me what you see."

At first I saw nothing, except that there were flowers by the stones. Little simple twists of pink and white blooms that whispered in the blue breeze. It was as if they had blown in on a tide.

"All men," I said, shrugging my shoulders. That was all that the names told me.

"All *young* men. In their twenties and thirties. And all of them died... by their own hands. They killed themselves because their way of life was gone and they didn't know what to do. They were told they could be bank managers and pilots and engineers – but they couldn't be. They went south and got everything that money could buy. They gained the whole world and lost their own souls. Why? Because of this!" He bent down and tore up the moss and heather by his foot with trembling fingers. "Because the land, the reindeer, they were asleep in their blood, they were part of their very heartbeat." He let the moss be carried by the breeze. "And what next? Will there be another generation of Sami at all or will they vanish? If the language dies and the herding culture is forgotten then what do we become? A costume for tourists? Nothing more than a book in which our story is written, a book whose ink is slowly fading? When do a people cease to exist? When do they lose the last of their identity?" He smiled. "I must stop this bleakness. Come and I will take you to meet Magga."

She was the oldest woman in the Karasjok community;

an old tortoise who carried the shell of her back painfully but whose eyes slid sideways at the world like new-cut gems. In the early afternoon we sat with our backs to a long curve of the river, a creature low and silted and sleepy with the weight of summer, and rolled ourselves cigarettes as the mosquitoes swivelled and hummed in the still air. England and Sweden were playing football and Magga's son, Jostein, and Lars were rooting madly for England. Anyone who could humiliate Sweden was to be applauded. Now and again one of them would turn the dial of a radio that lay splayed in the grass to listen to the score. The silence crackled as a finger rolled the dial to find the huge waves of songs, the sound of clapping, the high-pitched singsong of a Norwegian commentator. It was a place so far away it no longer mattered to me; it was a journey on foot, then by car, then three days by steamer, before a final drive home. But it was further away even than that...

Magga asked me if I knew how the Sami had survived.

I sat up in the grass and shook my head. She told Lars in a long string of toothless sentences that were interspersed with gestures and a stamped foot, and finally ended with folded arms. The eyes swivelled to see if I had been listening and Lars translated.

"By the early 1970s the Sami were a broken people. Our language was more or less illegal and could not be taught in school – the whole process of 'Scandivisation' was all but complete. The Norwegian government decided to build a dam in the Alta valley, a place held sacred by the Sami for centuries. It was the last straw that broke the camel's back – or perhaps the last branch that broke the reindeer's back, you might say. The Sami, especially the young, came

in their native costume and chained themselves to the diggers. They came in their thousands. It still looked a desperate and pathetic struggle. But then the international media
got wind of it and they descended with their whole circus
on Alta. They asked questions: who were the Sami and
why were they being persecuted? Why was this valley being
flooded if the people did not want it? The Scandinavians,
the great ambassadors for peace and justice everywhere
from Cambodia to South Africa, were suddenly discovered
with blood on their own hands at their very back door. It
brought about a sea change was brought about that has
lasted to this day. Linguistic and cultural rights, justice for
the reindeer herders, new laws against discrimination..."

Jostein suddenly squealed, his ear buried in the froth-
ing of the radio. "England have scored! England have
scored!" Lars and he howled with joy and, for a moment,
the history of their struggle for self-determination was
forgotten in a long, warm babble of Sami delight. Even
Magga's eyes disappeared in her face under wrinkles as she
smiled.

Lars sat up again at last, his hair tousled. "After Alta,
the little Lapplander dared to grow up. But was it the end
of the beginning or the beginning of the end? Remember
what I told you in the graveyard."

The match ended and the radio lay silent on its back
in the grass. Magga said she had something in the house
she wanted me to drink. It was clear that I should follow
her as she went awkwardly up from the riverbank towards
the house. It is strange to walk alongside a human being
with whom you cannot communicate at all – silence is
loud and odd. Her kitchen smelled of flies and dogs. I

was a stranded island in the middle of the uneven floor as she padded round, opening cupboards and cooking something that smelled sour and burnt. She sat me down at the table and presented me with coffee so thick it looked as if it could fill holes in the farm track. In another bowl in front of me were hot oval lumps of something white that smelled distinctly goaty. Lars and Jostein came in grinning like jackals, hands in their jeans as they stood by the table watching.

"Reindeer cheese," said Lars. "Be sure and take lots of sugar."

The cheese balls plopped into the coffee with three swivelfuls of sugar. I blew and drank. It tasted appalling, utterly revolting, and I wondered if I was going to manage to keep it down at all.

"Lovely," I gulped, "it's lovely!" and the three of them rocked on their heels, laughing. Their narrow eyes disappeared in their dark faces as they laughed at me tenderly, like parents at their child.

An hour later Magga fell asleep in her chair and Lars and I slipped away into the still blue glow of the afternoon.

"I have arranged a journey for you, with the only pilot in Karasjok – my brother-in-law! He'll take you right into the heart of Sami country – 250 miles from anywhere."

He left me on an edge of forest near his brother-in-law's house where the family was building a cabin. Mikkel hardly greeted me as he staggered past with a heaped hod of bricks, finished digging a channel and threw instructions to his own father watching on the edge of the plot. The old man was covered in mosquitoes; his whole face crawled with them so his features appeared to be part of some lunatic Dali or Picasso portrait, constantly changing and melting and disappearing.

The wood was so still you could have heard a pin drop in Moscow; the mosquitoes sang and whizzed, the midnight air was hot and lemon. The very pines seemed to sweat their resin and I stood there fighting the mosquitoes with my arms like one drowning while the old man smiled at me triumphantly, the edges of his mouth twisted and buried by a boiling of mosquitoes. It was said by the Sami that you could always recognise strangers because they were the only ones who ever fought the mosquitoes.

We went down to Mikkel's seaplane in the end. It lay like a white insect in a backwater of the river and Mikkel's two young twin sons bounded ahead of us, falling and yapping. They scrambled like cubs into the back of the plane as we hummed out along the river and rose up at last in a clear curve into the luminous Lappland night to meet the last embers of the sun. It lay in a rose bonfire to the west of the world, out on the rim of the sea, and suddenly I saw Hammerfest too, hunched up in the boxes of its fish sheds and its own stink. Karasjok trailed away behind us, nothing more than a cluster of wooden cabins beside a river.

But now the plane was rippled by sunlight and our faces doused in a midnight light like liquid apples. It touched a thousand cups of lakes in the tundra beneath, turned it into a waterland across which the reindeer battled in silver herds. They ran ahead of us, almost as if they were leading us inexorably into their kingdom. And the plane itself showed against the eastern hillsides like a single midge, its drone the only noise in the vastness of that world of moor and lake and moor; and somehow in that moment this little midge became a metaphor for all that we were and represented amid the vast cathedral of that wilderness.

We came down in a single sweep and breathed out over a piece of water that stretched as far as the eye could see. When we climbed down across the skis and jumped over onto the heathery rocks of the shore I was aware more than anything else of the extraordinary noise in my ears. I had never been further from humanity in all my life: Karasjok, Kautokeino, Lakselv and Hammerfest were all beyond the edges of the sky. Fifty miles on every side there was nothing but moor and lake and moor. I had imagined such a place would be composed of utter and complete tranquillity, and to my surprise it was made of nothing but noise.

The trumpeting of whooper and mute swans, the take-offs and landings of 10,000 geese, the bubbling of grebes and phalarope and divers, a polyphony of warblers and linnets and buntings. I stood there, in the middle of a song that had been sung every summer since the creation – unchanged. It was the oldest thing I had encountered in all my life. I looked at Mikkel and his boys, playing together like bears on the windswept ground, part of their kingdom still – its inheritors.

TWO

John Cunningham

The Sami people weren't always confined to the north of Scandinavia. Evidence of their settlements showed they had a presence – in Norway – as far south as Oslo. The reason for their retreat was conflict with the Scandinavian settlers; their respective cultures (and languages) were radically different, and it was all too easy for suspicion to lead to misunderstanding. The settlers had power on their side; in time they had the law too. When it came to both, the Sami would be losers – time and time again. That further fuelled resentment.

Norway, Sweden and Finland decided finally on their northern borders; I often think, as an analogy, of how the "plates" of a baby's head at last knit together for good. They all played the game of taxing the Sami; sometimes communities would be paying to more than one authority. The whole silliness of borders in this part of the high Arctic is brought home best when one steps out of a car and takes in the full extent of the emptiness. This is how it has been for an unthinkably long time: a tundra landscape extending for hundreds of miles, knowing no human disturbance and – especially in the long hours of the summer light – nothing more than the calls of curlew and phalarope and grebe.

But the Scandinavian settlers had a good idea of what was to be found here by way of natural resources. They particularly wanted to exploit populations of wolf, lynx, bear and wolverine – and these were abundant in this great northern wilderness. The problem was that this was the Sami heartland, and though the settlers might often entertain strange ideas about their neighbours to the north, they were very aware of the reality of their shamanism.

It was all very well showing the Sami who was boss with their law books, but legislating against magic was something even they hadn't learned to do. There seems to have been a particular fear of unnatural storms and strange winds being conjured and sent by Sami magicians, but there seems to have been a *general* fear of going too far and risking the consequences of shamanic practice. The settlers most likely knew that it was certain Sami men who had to be feared in particular, for women were not privy to the magic arts of the *noaddi*, or shaman.

It was this fear of shamanism that, in part at least, led to the unlikely scenario of a Scotsman who hailed from the East Neuk of Fife, not far from St Andrews, being appointed district governor of Finnmark province (the northernmost county of Norway) at the beginning of the 17th century. It was the Danes who made the appointment, for at that time Norway was ruled from Copenhagen: Denmark-Norway existed as a single country.

John Cunningham was born around 1575. King Christian IV, who had known Scots before and had found good reason to trust them, gave him command of a naval ship that was to sail to Greenland with two other vessels. The king wanted to flex his northern muscles; it was important for him that pirates and marauders were shown who was ruling the roost on the high seas around his territories. He also wanted Cunningham to bring back Inuit prisoners who could be displayed like zoo animals in Copenhagen. So it was that on this expedition in 1605 Cunningham shot dead one of the four Inuit who had been captured: it seems the poor souls had gone berserk on board the vessel and, as a warning to the others, Cunningham had killed him. Different times, indeed. It was this very ruthlessness that so impressed the Danish king: John Cunningham had displayed his courage in other ways too, and in 1619 was rewarded by being appointed district governor of the province of Finnmark. He held the post until his death in 1651: quite an extraordinarily long time.

It's pretty obvious that John Cunningham was the right man for the job. But it wasn't just sheer ruthlessness and the wielding of strong authority that won him respect and kept him on the Finnmark "throne". To begin with, he wasn't the only Scot in the province. There appear to have been a whole string of Scottish settler families along that northernmost coast of Norway, some of them so established that they had been rewarded with positions of one kind or another. How they ended up there is another matter: it has to be remembered just how far north of the Arctic Circle this is, and how demanding the winters are. There's total darkness for several months: not greyness, not half-light – total and complete midnight darkness. On the northern coast of Norway, there's nothing to protect communities from the utter ferocity of the storms.

But one must assume that Cunningham would have forged contact with these fellow Scots, particularly those who had won some status in their adopted country. So Cunningham wasn't a total fish out of water. He also seems to have been blessed with brains as well as brawn; during his years in Finnmark he appears to have acquired a number of languages – valuable, indeed necessary, when sitting surrounded by all of these different ethnic communities and their various needs and demands.

King Christian IV may well have wanted Cunningham to break down the power of the Sami: fear of shamanism was so strong that the Scandinavian settlers simply wouldn't move to certain locations in Finnmark. But weakening the Sami was more easily said than done. As long as taxes were paid and their own way of life was carried on peacefully, the Sami couldn't really be blamed. It was only when flash-points arose that intervention was possible.

Cunningham must have known all about the North Berwick witch trials of 1590–91. North Berwick was across the Firth of Fife from where he had grown up, and by then he would have been in his teens. He left behind a country that was in the grip of witch fever; Scotland's King James VI (and I of England) was positively obsessed with the subject and even wrote a book about it.

It seems that previous district governors simply hadn't locked horns with Sami sorcery before. Records show that during Cunningham's time of office in Finnmark there were fifty-two witch trials; there may have been more that were not recorded. Yet only nine of these were of Sami individuals: the remainder involved Norwegians. But for such a sparsely populated region, that's a high number of trials.

And those found guilty, whether Sami or Norwegian, male or female, faced the same fate as their counterparts elsewhere in Europe.

Yet if it made a difference, it can't have been huge. One is left feeling that for all his years in power, Cunningham wasn't very successful in breaking that Sami hold over the inner part of Finnmark in particular. And *this* was the important part. The next centuries would find the authorities employing all manner of new pieces of legislation and new ways of wielding power in an attempt to break that hold.

THREE

A Shamanic World

Shamanism has not only been a feature of the regions populated by the Sami; the Arctic as a whole has been a shamanic world. Perhaps in pockets, and in times of need, it still is. The landscape, with its places of ancient strangeness, was important to that framework of understanding: a rock emerging from the tundra was seen as a figure frozen there after some battle with dark forces; a river emerging from the earth was considered sacred. Perhaps these things were all the more important because in the main the landscape is hauntingly unchanging – a stranger would be lost in minutes because there are so few defining features.

In Greenland the sea was very obviously of huge signif icance. Out of it came an abundance of fish, seals, narwhal and whales. Reaping a rich harvest from the sea would mean the difference between survival and death when everything was dictated by a raging winter that lasted all but half the year. Sedna governed that harvest; she sat at the mouth of her cave on the seabed with her long black hair. Once upon a time a hunter had cut off her fingers; now she was no longer able to untangle her hair or pull from it the creatures trapped there.

The shaman worked himself (and almost invariably it would be a man) into a trance through the beating of a drum. He then descended on his spirit journey into the sea and down to the ocean floor and Sedna's cave. Here he would comb her matted hair and free it of all that was trapped there before returning to the upper world and those he had left.

The problem was that once didn't suffice; Sedna's hair would return to its former state and the task had to be completed over and over again. That sense of the constant need to appease the spirits, to keep fulfilling their wishes, seems common to the Arctic peoples; in fact, fear lies almost like a bedrock in every one.

And the shaman was often an immensely feared figure. The power of the evil eye is described time and time again. These men held sway over their communities; if they chose to exert that power and allowed themselves to be consumed by it, who would ever dare stand against them?

I lived in Arctic Norway towards the end of the 1980s: to this day I wish I had visited Tysfjord at that time; there was still no proper roads in, and the district remained pretty much a southern Sami enclave. The students admitted there was someone in the community they were afraid of, someone who used what they called "the black book". I heard from colleagues of a student from Tysfjord who had been at the college in earlier years and who simply seemed to carry a dark power. It was as though he cast a shadow over the place until, after some weeks, there was a decisive and traumatic confrontation and he was expelled. Everyone I spoke to maintained it was as though the sun came out again from behind the clouds.

All of this is extremely difficult to write about in such a rationalist, sceptical age. But I want to make it clear that the reports and the stories are unthinkably many, and that they have existed all down the centuries. When back in northern Norway conducting the research for this book, I found a slim paperback in Alta's library on ghost stories and accounts of possessions; these were not from the dim and distant past – they were all from the last *twenty years*.

Cunningham, the governor from Fife in Scotland, to whom the previous chapter is devoted, did capture a few *noaddi* during his years in Finnmark. Witch trials and burnings were raging across Europe; here in the Sami world it was very much men who were sent to the stake. Nonetheless, I don't have the sense that he ever really managed to break into that world as the ruling Danes must have hoped. This was a region that went on being feared in a very real way; even travel by land and sea was done with trepidation because of the storms it was believed could be cast by the shamen.

In other parts of the Arctic beyond Greenland the shaman also beat a drum to descend into the realm of the spirits. But here the purpose was to carry back messages for the living; there was no task that had to be performed beyond that. The rune drum was a simple enough construction; a round frame of wood over which was stretched a taut skin. The surface of that skin had drawn onto it all manner of totem creatures and figures: at the very heart was often a representation of the sun. Without the sun there could be no life, and what was more precious than light in a northern world where the sun was totally absent for three or four months?

A Sami shaman would sing *joik* to work himself into a trance for the journey to the spirit world. A *joik* is almost invariably composed of sounds rather than actual words; sometimes one single song can last up to half an hour or longer. But *joik* was by no means solely concerned with this spirit journey by the *noaddi*; it encompassed the whole of living. Often *joik* were – and are – sung in the great outdoors. There were all manner of places that were seen as sacred; often, as has been mentioned, because of some peculiarity of "birth" – a cliff or a strange-shaped boulder, an island on a lake or the formation of a hill top. *Joik* would be sung here to celebrate the story of the place, to remember family past and present, to rejoice in the return of spring, to give thanks for the finding of love. In other words *joik* was about every part of human experience.

The missionaries simply associated it with the trance of the shaman and considered it to be of the Devil. *Joik* was illegal in Norway until remarkably recently, though for obvious reasons that did not mean it disappeared. But the Sami community is still sharply and painfully divided between the Christian and the not. That latter part remembers a time when anything Sami was seen as wrong, backward and even wicked. At the time of working on this book in Alta, a row was raging over whether or not *joik* could be sung in the church in Kautokeino. Somehow that seemed to say it all.

One of the totem animals that might appear on the rune drum was the bear. The wolf was seen as an evil creature (much as in Western culture generally), but the bear was considered holy. Right the way from the Sami in Arctic Scandinavia to the Ainu people in the north of Japan, all the native groups whose origins had been Mongolian and who practised shamanism, believed in the bear as "God's creature".

Often their veneration of the bear involved a ritualistic spring sacrifice. The women stayed behind to prepare the dwelling place for the return of the hunters. The men most likely worked out beforehand the hibernating bear that was to be killed. The creature was driven out and slaughtered; the man who delivered the fatal blow was considered honoured during the year that followed. Often a special carved chair was set aside for him. It was as though he had absorbed the bear's spirit and power – its very holiness.

A few years ago I was asked to open an exhibition of Inuit art in Caithness in the north of Scotland. It was an odd assemblage of artefacts, mainly composed of carvings. The piece that struck me most vividly was of a hunter raising a spear against a roaring polar bear. I looked at it for a long time, became quite mesmerised by the superb skill of the carver who had created something that seemed almost alive. It was as though you could hear the roar both of hunter and bear. And then I looked again and saw the power that somehow travelled between the two; it was hard to say where the roar and the forward lunge of the bear ended or the thrust of the hunter's spear began. It is more than mere killing; it is about an exchange and absorption of spirit.

As I have said, this veneration of the bear continued all the way across to the north of Japan and the Ainu. There, in former times, they captured a cub and kept it almost like a living teddy bear, as something for their children to play with. Then, after a year of being pampered and fattened, the creature was killed.

It's difficult to know what is to be found today in terms of traditional belief and practice across the Arctic, because so much of what remains of an older culture – if it remains at all – is likely to have gone underground.

The church has made more of an attempt to identify with indigenous culture where once it would have been seen as colluding with the state in frowning on it at best and suffocating it at worst. That would seem a little too late; a fairly recent reversal of attitudes cannot undo long centuries of prejudice. Yet the Arctic communities have long had strong Christian attachments, and it's not hard to see why a core message of hope and light would have been attractive to people whose lives were governed by constant fear of the spirit world and of those who acted as intermediaries.

And the truth is that a lot of the old ways have been forgotten. What remains is like the tattered remnants of a garment stretched pathetically thinly across the Arctic world; it has been torn over and over again, and most of it is lost forever.

FOUR

Lars Levi Laestadius

In the year 1800 Lars Levi Laestadius was born into a troubled family: this is not merely a footnote for interest's sake, it was of huge significance for the course of his life. His father was a Swede and something of a jack of all trades, but his life was defined by alcohol – and ruined by it. Consequently Lars Levi grew up in great poverty, and with a boiling anger at the poison that had destroyed his father's life and ruined his family.

Lars Levi's mother was a southern Sami, and that was most significant for his future life too. He learned the Sami language alongside Swedish, and he was a brilliant scholar. Although it was to be theology that took centre stage in the years that followed, it was botany that he studied first.

It seems that Lars Levi Laestadius became a dedicated priest who knew the right theological arguments. But at this stage it was all head rather than heart. At the age of twenty-six Laestadius went north to the Karesuando district at the very roof of Sweden. It was a region in meltdown. At the heart of the misery lay alcohol; the whole way of life was breaking down, with reindeer being sold and whole communities falling apart. Laestadius must have been all too aware of the situation as a priest in the midst of all the misery.

In 1844 Laestadius was to have a meeting with a Sami woman that would change the course of his life and, effectively, the Sami world as a whole. Oddly enough, it was almost a Damascus Road experience, for, as has been stated, he was first and foremost a religious scholar at that time. The woman told him about her journey to living faith, and the priest underwent a conversion experience that did nothing less than set fire to his life.

At the heart of the new man was a profound love of his own people. He saw himself as a Sami, and what he yearned for more than anything was to bring his people back from the brink. He had seen what alcohol had done to his own family and he had seen at first-hand how it had reduced the northern Sami world to near ruin. He had to preach against alcohol so the people saw how it was fragmenting their families and communities.

But it was the particular ingredients of Laestadius' missionary zeal that made all the difference. Suspicion of settled Scandinavian society was at an all-time high: it was, after all, this society that was selling spirits to the Sami with little or no regard for the consequences. The fact that Laestadius was seen to be from the Sami world was of huge importance. The fact that he spoke not one but two Sami dialects was of real significance. And the fact that he loved his traditional Sami world and wanted it to survive was simply vital.

That meant he endorsed the Sami way of life. The timing was crucial, for that way of life was breaking down and unravelling fast. Laestadius was *for* their Sami dress, he was *for* their language, he was *for* the old world that had been theirs for countless centuries. What he did not endorse, fairly obviously, were shamanic practices – still very much being used. Those had to be left behind, but more than anything else it was the bottle that had to be put down once and for all.

Lars Levi succeeded also because his sermons took their metaphors from everyday Sami society. They were about a world people understood, that they knew and which made sense. He was also wise enough to employ fellow missionaries who were not outsiders but rather reindeer herders themselves. They spoke the same language – literally and metaphorically speaking.

It was said of Laestadius' missionary activity that it "ran like heather fires through the land". He was like a latter-day St Paul, especially when one considers the kind of area he covered to preach. Vast distances lay between scattered communities, but Laestadius had found his purpose and nothing was going to hold him back. His life was plagued by illness and he lost family members in miserably quick succession; no one is quite certain how many of his own twelve children succumbed. It is as though he took up the faded, broken garment that composed the Sami land, and bound it together with a melding of anger and sheer love.

What happened was little short of a miracle. It's said to this day that communities became "dry" overnight. And the pews were set alight with the zeal with which Lars Levi fired them. What is most moving is that these communities found a dignity for themselves that had been lost. Drunkenness diminished or disappeared altogether, which had a positive effect on relationships, finances and family life.

Religious movements tend to be known for their schisms. Pathetically futile squabbles will erupt over the interpretation of the smallest and narrowest of theological contentions. Laestadius' church was little different. Four branches of the denomination that came to bear his name resulted in the end. But the importance of its original mission is undisputed. And to this day it is the Laestadian Church that is at the heart of the Christian Sami world.

* * *

But there is an ugly, though necessary, postscript to the story of Laestadius and his mission. He was responsible for a revival, not only within the church but within wider Sami society. Almost inevitably revival of this kind is set to create division and tension. At the height of this frenetic criss-crossing of the Sami heartland with his message, Laestadius was loved and loathed in equal measure.

What happened in Kautokeino in early November 1852 cast a shadow over the whole revival, both in its time and to this very day. A group of some thirty-five Sami converts, led by two men by the names of Aslak Haetta and Mons Somby, marched on the town. They were fired up by the message of Laestadius as they came over the Swedish border into Norway from Karesuando. The town of Kautokeino lies strategically placed deep in the heart of inland Finnmark, relatively close to the point where the three Arctic countries meet. To this day, Kautokeino is a solidly Sami community, and composed first and foremost of reindeer herders. The group of revivalists were full of religious fervour and had come to the town as crusaders "to wage war on the unrepentant". In particular they were seeking out one shopkeeper who had been selling spirits. During the riot that ensued, they killed the shopkeeper and burned down his home. They also killed the local policeman. They did not approve of the priest in the town either, so he was beaten up and an attempt was made to burn down the church. Some of the rioters fled to the hills around Kautokeino to try to escape the long arm of the law, but most were captured. Aslak Haetta and Mons Somby, the leaders of the group, were beheaded. One of the others was imprisoned for many years and used his time in jail to work on the first translation of the Bible into northern Sami. The skulls of the two men who were beheaded were taken for detailed scientific examination.

What emerges from the dust of the Kautokeino Uprising are the clear sides of a debate that rages to this day: was the revival that Laestadius set alight for good or for ill? It's clear that what he did to break the hold that *spirits* had on the Sami community was undoubtedly necessary and in the nick of time: the remnants of the old Sami world might well have been almost literally washed away without such intervention. It was enormously important that he endorsed Sami language and culture, thus restoring pride in what was often viewed from the outside as backward and of little or no worth. It's a fact that what Laestadius set in motion meant that the outside community began to view more respectfully Sami identity and culture. None of that can be doubted.

But, on the other hand, it caused desperate divisions, fault lines that have become more pronounced with the passing of the decades. The church has been hated by many Sami, first and foremost because it has been considered nothing less than an arm of the state. And it was, and is, a state church. It said far too little about the worst repression of Sami language and culture during the second half of the 19th century and the first half of the 20th century. The branch of the church that bears the name of Laestadius feels very out of touch with the modern world: it still endorses the language and culture of its people – up to a point – but one could argue there has been little or no evolution in its thinking since the days of its founder.

When she was growing up, the Sami singer Mari Boine infamously burned her Bible as a protest. Perhaps it would be correct to say that it was more a protest against the church than against Christianity, though that's ultimately for Mari Boine to say. When one visits the various corners of the Sami heartland one is almost immediately aware of the stark division between those who are church members and those who would struggle to darken a church door.

Yet all that can be said is that what is left of the church in the far north would seem to have done its utmost to make up for the collusion with the state in earlier times. There at the Easter services in Karasjok, at the time this book was being put together, was a priest originally from the east of Norway who had poured his life into his service of the Sami community: his fluency in the Sami language was testament to that. Perhaps the fight over Alta was a wake-up call to the church as it was to the people in the streets: it would seem only fair to say – if you'll forgive the expression – that in terms of Sami justice the church is on the side of the angels now.

Above: Karasjok, Norway. *Below*: Spring ice, Inari, Finland.

Above: The Sami Parliament building, Inari, Finland.

Opposite (top): Outside Karasjok.

Below and opposite (bottom): The Sami Museum, Karasjok, Norway.

Above and opposite: In traditional dress, Karasjok.

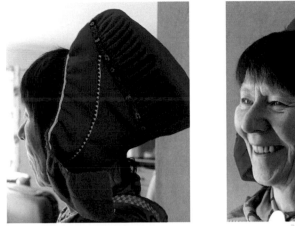

All photographs © Kristina Hayward

Above: (left) A traditional Sami drum, Sami Museum, Karasjok.

Above: (right) Window detail, Sami Parliament, Karasjok.

Opposite: The road to Kautokeino.

Below: The old church in Karasjok.

All photographs © Kristina Hayward

Above: Cloudberry.

Below: Evening light, Inari.

FIVE

The "Fornorsking" of the Sami

It's worth taking a finer lens to the story of forced Norwegenisation (or *fornorsking*, as it is in Norwegian) to understand the highly significant period of influence and change for the Sami between 1840 and 1960. For one thing, it makes the whole story of what came afterwards a great deal more meaningful. It's important too because the story needs to be nuanced and not composed of rather sweeping generalisations. There is a very definite evolution to that *fornorsking* process, much of it directly influenced by the political thinking of the time.

It's essential to remember that Norway wasn't even a fully independent country until 1905. Back in 1814 when the constitution was established, Norway was still part of Denmark. Instead of finding freedom in that momentous year, Norway was simply handed like a parcel to Sweden. The constitution was a wonderfully exciting document inspired by the ideals of the French Revolution and American independence. So in many ways it's of little surprise that the period after the establishment of the constitution in Norway was the most positive for the Sami. It was a time of idealism that placed the right to identity and language centre-stage: it was almost inevitable that the Sami would be seen in a new light. For the first time, for example, books were produced in the Sami language.

But 1851 marked an important deterioration in that new way of thinking about the Sami world and its language. What was established was called *finnefondet* – namely a fund to pay for the teaching of Norwegian to children in northern Norway who spoke Sami and Finnish as their respective mother tongues. From the end of the 1860s the *fornorsking* process was dramatically increased, mainly as a result of the migration of Finnish language speakers into East-Finnmark.

In 1880 a directive stated that all Sami and Finnish-speaking children should learn to read, write and count in Norwegian. Teachers who could demonstrate good results when it came to the carrying out of this policy would be given extra pay, and for many this meant a significant and tempting wage increase – as much as 20–30%.

In 1898 the final, toughest policy of all was implemented. Once again it was grounded in "the danger from the east" (in other words, the Finns), and it shows just how much the Sami-speaking communities suffered because of a primary fear of Finland. Now it was demanded that the use of Sami and Finnish be restricted to the absolute minimum, solely as a last resort to explain what was otherwise totally inexplicable to children. The directive also charged teachers with controlling the use of the two "foreign" tongues, seeing that they were not used during break times. Only a very few teachers would have had Sami or Finnish origins; there was general scepticism about employing such teachers.

At last Norway found full freedom, this time from Sweden, in 1905. The break-up of the union was of huge significance in building national pride and a sense of identity. That in turn had consequences for the whole *fornorsking* process. Now there was a new drive and initiative with the establishment of a host of boarding schools throughout Finnmark, the aim being the isolation of pupils from their home worlds. The authorities now deliberately chose Norwegian teachers for both Sami and Finnish-speaking districts; in other words there was a de facto ban on the employment of "native" teachers.

The next phase of development can be seen as taking place between 1905 and 1950. The Treaty of Versailles after the First World War changed the borders of the countries whose northernmost counties met in the region known as Nordkalotten: for Norway that resulted in a common border with Russia and Finland.

The building of boarding schools went on apace; Christian Brygfjeld was one of the most terrifying directors of education in this period (his "reign" being from 1923 to 1935). These were his words: "The Lapps have neither had the means nor the will to use their own language as a written tongue. The few individuals who remain from the original Lappish people are now so degenerate that there is little hope for any change for the better with them. They are hopeless and belong to Finnmark's most backwards and useless inhabitants." Of course, such views can be seen as linking in with much similar thinking of the time: it was hardly confined to Germany.

During this period there came to be a distinction in the way that the Sami and the Finnish-speaking minority were perceived. The Sami were seen as the lesser of the two because they were racially different and their origins inferior – in other words, they fell short.

The final stage of the *fornorsking* process occurred between 1950 and 1980. The boarding school conditions designed to keep Sami children deliberately away from their homes and the whole sphere of influence of their childhood districts continued into the 1960s.

The effect of *fornorsking* was, inevitably, the forcing of the Sami to be other than they were. It can be seen that this state campaign to get the Sami to put to one side their language, to change the basic values of their culture and to change their very identity had been long and clear in its aims. The psycho-social consequences were clear too: the long-term result of the policy would affect one's self-image, undermine self-respect and self-worth, and at worst lead to a denial of one's own identity, and to an exaggerated and over-critical perception of members of one's own community.

It's valuable to note that for a time the church was opposed to the whole *fornorsking* process. However, those who did oppose it were characterised as reactionaries who wanted to wander back to bewildered thinking about language in education, and fools who ignored the hard "fact" that *fornorsking* would elevate the Sami in material, cultural and religious terms.

The direct result of a sustained *fornorsking* policy over many decades is perhaps unsurprising: the Sami themselves began to look down on and even reject their own language and culture. The perception of a backward and worthless inheritance started to take hold. This recorded interview with an elderly Sami couple, from around 1915, speaks for itself:

"It's better to use the language that's spoken in Norway. This is a language that's dying out. What's the point of keeping it going? It's the old souls that can't walk any more that have Sami. And you lot at university who work to get the language up and running again. It's just rubbish!"

SIX

A Swedish Secret

There is a chapter of this whole story that belongs principally to Sweden, though it is hardly one the Swedes would want to acknowledge (and few would blame them). Yet ownership of the consequences has to be very much acknowledged by Denmark, Norway and Finland too.

At the heart of it all was a doctor by the name of Herman Lundborg. He was born in 1868 and received his doctorate from the University of Uppsala. Lundborg was obsessed by the whole idea of the racial purity of the Swedish people; it might be said that his very mission was, as he saw it, to save Sweden from racial degeneration. Although he was very much anti-Semitic, Lundborg's near obsession was with the Sami.

In 1922 the Swedish Institute for Eugenics was established: the first in the world. At its helm was Herman Lundborg. In 1926 studies conducted by the institute provided a basis for Lundborg's upper secondary school textbook, *Swedish Racial Studies*. Whatever else he was, Lundborg was an extraordinarily hard worker. Each and every summer – for several months – he went north to "map" Sami men, women and children. They were photographed and measured, both with and without clothing. Lundborg was particularly concerned with head size: for him it was all about those who had long skulls and those who had short.

A good number of his photographs were of people from a mixed racial background: his intention with these was to show their degeneration. The paradox is that the vast library of images of the Sami is a great record in and of itself, even though the purpose behind its creation was wholly negative. Many of the pictures are hauntingly beautiful. Perhaps it was that Lundborg's fascination for the Sami people became more than just about fear and suspicion: it's as though the north came to have a strong hold over him. Although he was married with a family in the south of Sweden, he met a woman from the far north who became an assistant on his field trips – a speaker of Sami. But at some point their relationship must have deepened; they had a child together and, in the wake of his wife's death, he married this girl from the north, and in the fullness of time she was buried with him.

Herman Lundborg himself fell out of favour with the Swedish government during the 1930s as tensions grew between Sweden and Germany; his strong anti-Semitic stance would have been of significance here. Nonetheless, during the years of his research, Lundborg mapped the racial make-up of a staggering 100,000 Swedes. And his work went on to be important far beyond Sweden; he himself felt a natural kinship with Germany during the pre-war years, and his findings were very much taken on board by the regime. Not only that, but his *techniques* were learned and employed by the emerging Nazi dictatorship.

Paradoxically enough, in later years his work became of interest to the Soviets too. And his whole way of thinking was by no means seen as incredible or even dangerous at that time: the classic American novel *The Great Gatsby* by F Scott Fitzgerald is proof enough of that. The principal characters in the story talk with excitement about a book that has been published on the survival of the white race and the dangers of creating a racial cocktail to degenerate that white purity. Far from being disturbed or frightened by the book's message, the main protagonists of Fitzgerald's work seem quite excited by it.

All that having been said, Lundborg's research was finally discredited in Sweden (despite it being cited and used elsewhere). He himself was replaced at the helm of the institute in 1936 by Gunnar Dahlberg. But although he was replaced, it certainly did not mean that the general way of thinking changed. This central fear of the degeneration of the Swedish race remained, that it could also occur because of mental illness, addiction and criminality. The laws to enable a preventative programme were passed by the new Social Democratic government in 1934. The intention would appear to have been the saving of the cost of welfare for those deemed to be degenerate.

Sweden was later shocked to the core to discover that between 1935 and 1975 some 60,000 women were sterilised. Across the water in Denmark there had been 11,000 over a similar period of time, and in Norway and Finland 1,000 respectively. Of course the statistic from Sweden towers above the rest: just how had doctors gone alone with this programme? How much had people known and were there no dissenting voices? The truth is that these and many other questions surrounding a fully-fledged eugenics programme have not been formally asked and certainly not answered. My own knowledge of Lundborg's research among the Sami came from an excellent documentary on Swedish television made in 2014. But a thorough scouring of the Internet on the subject turns up all too little.

I want to finish with what I consider to be a fascinating postscript bringing all this back to Scotland. I have long had a great interest in the Scottish travelling people: I grew up in the heart of their country in rural Perthshire. In the course of interviews with two prominent women from the traveller community for BBC Radio, I noted with considerable interest their mention of something that has become a folk memory. During the early part of the last century, someone visited that traveller community to examine them and conduct measurements. I wonder if there was once a Scottish Herman Lundborg, travelling the north of the country and working every bit as hard.

SEVEN

Alta

In a sense everything leads to Alta, the struggle that is of such central importance to the Sami – and in symbolic terms to indigenous peoples right across the world. Thirty years on, it is still the consequences of the Alta campaign that the Sami are building on, certainly in Norway. After centuries of state-sanctioned discrimination, this was what began to change everything.

It was the pictures I first saw back in the early 1980s that sowed those first seeds of fascination. But the roots of the story really go a good deal deeper, to 1971 and the first plans for the construction of a dam. From the outset I want to acknowledge Lars Martin Hjorthol and his excellent book on the Alta story (*Alta – kraftkampen som utfordret statens makt*, or "Alta – the power struggle that challenged state power"). When I was back in Arctic Norway, working away at the research for this book, I spent most days in Alta library. Outside it was often twenty-below and barely light at all; it was still the end of *mørketiden* – when the sun is not to be seen during the long winter months. But in the library I was accorded a real welcome; I had wanted to be based here precisely because I reckoned there would be specialist material on the story of the dam and all that happened in its wake. That, indeed, turned out to be the case. Despite the wonders of the Internet and the easy exchange of electronic material, I found that the library contained local books with exactly the kind of focus on the story that I sought. There is a special section of the library devoted to books on Sami culture and language (as there should be: this is the heart of northern Sami country). But of all the material I found, that work by Lars Martin was by far and away the most valuable. It was in Norwegian, so I worked my way through it in order to be able to reconstruct the skeletal framework of the story in English. So my thanks to him for an invaluable piece of work.

He was the best person to write this account, for he himself was one of the protestors. It so happened that the headmaster of the Folk High School close to Alta where I stayed for over a month to work on the gathering of the material for this book had been a protestor too. He was kind enough to bring me in to his office on a busy day and tell me something of what it had been like to be part of the campaign. The building of the dam had brought him to Arctic Norway – and he had never gone south again.

But why should the story of the building of a dam be given such attention? Is it somehow a case of the tail wagging the dog? No, not only did it change the Sami world forever, it also fundamentally changed Norwegian society. The protest over the building of the Alta dam all but brought down a government. It rocked the Norwegian royal family, and it made every ordinary Norwegian re-evaluate the way they perceived the Sami, who hitherto had been little more to them than a rather oddly clad minority wandering about with reindeer. If the truth be told.

* * *

In 1971 the Norwegian government's eyes were on a tiny Sami settlement by the name of Masi, lying between Alta and Kautokeino. It's one of the most fundamentally Sami communities there is in Norway: back then there were 400 inhabitants, all Sami speakers. The plans being drawn up in 1971 were for the creation of a 56-km long artificial lake between Alta and Kautokeino: the people of Masi would be forced to move and the settlement would be flooded.

It is important to make clear that there had been no real protests by the Sami before this time: the usual response over disputes, large and small, was for them to back off and obey the state. But generations of Sami had experienced both open and more subtle discrimination, and this drip-drip effect had taken its toll. Of course there was resentment; it lay beneath the surface like the poison in a boil. All the same, three years after the drawing up of those first plans, the Oslo parliament decided that Masi would be spared. Perhaps they realised that the flooding of the settlement would be unwise politically. At the same time, a debate was raging about who owned these vast tracts of "wilderness": was it the state (as the state itself claimed), or had centuries of use by the Sami given them the right to declare it theirs? So Masi had been saved, but the government had by no means ceased to have aspirations for the creation of a hydro-electric scheme between Alta and Kautokeino.

Gro Harlem Brundtland was minister for the environment in 1974. There were several potential hydro-electric schemes on the cards – of which Alta was one. It was important for her to show that the Norwegian Labour Party, her party, took the environment seriously. But the young and ambitious Brundtland (who would go on to serve three terms as Norway's prime minister) picked Hardanger in the southern, central part of Norway as the cause she was going to adopt. There was good reason to choose Hardanger: to begin with it was familiar to a far larger sector of Norwegian society. It was a classically beautiful area, popular for skiing and outdoor pursuits in general, and a holiday destination for many. The truth is that Alta in Finnmark – and the remote north in general – was way off the radar to the majority of the country's population, who lived down in Trondheim, Bergen and Oslo.

There has been much speculation in hindsight about Gro Harlem Brundtland's stance on Alta: the truth is that she said nothing about it at the time, didn't enter the fray at all. What seems likely to me is that from the beginning she saw Alta as a lost cause, and ambitious politicians don't adopt lost causes.

But what of opinion in Alta itself, and in Finnmark generally? It was all very well worrying about the attitudes of politicians a thousand miles south in the capital, but what about people on the ground where it counted? In truth, local political groups were split over the whole question of the building of the hydro-electric scheme: most were against, but not all. Alternatives were seen as too expensive and thus not truly viable. The governing Labour Party didn't view the damming of the Alta River as controversial; as they saw it, Sami concerns over Masi had been addressed. No one had any idea just what a huge cause it was to become.

* * *

The campaign against the Alta dam began in earnest on 12th July 1978, half a year after the Oslo parliament decided the scheme should be given the go-ahead. Somewhere in the region of eighty folk turned up for the meeting (little did anyone know that one day it would have become a protest group with 20,000 members and dedicated local groups all across the country). The embryonic group worked hard to gather evidence relating to the prospective damage to the environment – in particular to salmon numbers in the Alta River.

What is important to stress is that at this point it was very much a green campaign: the question of Sami rights was simply not raised at all, had no part in the debate. Little love was lost between northern Norwegian communities and the Sami: at best they were wary of each other. At the same time, the first protestors knew it was imperative to get the Sami "on side"; it was crucial that this was not just a cause adopted and fought by southern Norwegians. So the first rabble-rousing was done in Masi and in the pre-dominantly Sami community of Karasjok at the very heart of the Sami "highlands".

A turning point for the campaign came on 16th January 1979. Around 250 people gathered in Alta to discuss how best to fight parliament's decision: essentially they wanted to explore the taking of non-violent direct action. This was quite something. Here were people who'd rarely, if ever, had a parking ticket. But now they were considering openly breaking the law for the first time in their lives.

There were good reasons for the timing of this. Norway had a strong and radical young green movement, eager to be actively engaged, not just involved in endless debate. This was a tangible cause in their own country. It was also of huge significance to young and radical Sami especially: this was their territory, in every sense of the word.

It was crucial not just that the Sami were involved in the struggle, but that the campaign was seen to be spearheaded from Alta. The two things went hand in glove. If environmentalists down in Oslo appeared to be orchestrating things, it would cease to be a northern Norwegian cause – which it was – and one that very much centred on Sami rights. Nevertheless, the rest of the country and the opposition they mounted – wherever it was to be found – had to be harnessed and secured too. For that reason, local groups of activists were established up and down the country. This was going to prove of very real significance in the days to come.

The first real confrontation between the two sides – demonstrators and police – came on 5th July 1979. It was at a place called Stilla, about 20km from Alta Airport. This was the spot that had been given the name Ground Zero. It was here the engineers wanted to extend an existing road to lead to the planned power station. Around thirty campaigners sat in front of the diggers. From the outset the leaders of the campaign liaised with the police, partly to get them to realise that they were absolutely committed to the cause, but also to assure them that it was going to be about non-violent direct action and nothing else. None of their members was to think of throwing a punch, far less a brick.

But it wasn't as simple as police versus protestors. There was also a local group in favour of the building of the dam; they tore down posters and generally created as much noise as they could. Although there was never open confrontation between the opposing factions, the pro-dam campaigners remained a constant menace. Nonetheless, it was the other side that drew first blood: the local police force was way too weak to oust protestors from where they sat blocking access to the digging equipment. Over the next weeks and months, the protestors began to set about creating a camp, far north of the Arctic Circle, that would stand up to a winter in Norway's northernmost county.

Meanwhile, down in Oslo, on 8th October, a group of young Sami activists erected a *lavvo* (one of their traditional tents and closely related to the Native American wigwam) right in front of the parliament buildings. The group delivered a letter to the then prime minister, Odvar Nordli, stating that the building of the Alta dam had to stop to allow all Sami issues involved in the case to be explored. There had to be a response to the letter before noon on 9th October, and if nothing by way of a response materialised, the group would go on hunger strike.

And so they waited. There was no response to the letter, so they began their hunger strike as threatened. The *lavvo* action – as it now became known – grew into something truly major, quite possibly of even greater significance than the demonstrators ever believed possible. The young activists had all been denied the right to their own language at school: they were angry and they were extremely determined. They saw themselves as part of an international movement of exploited peoples. The cause was not just

Alta: it was the very future of the Sami. The hunger strike and the publicity it generated acted like the detonation of some kind of explosive device in the Norwegian consciousness. This persecution of native people should be a sheer impossibility, yet here was a Sami *lavvo* right in front of their own parliament in the capital, and the message coming out of it said something quite different.

There were now huge demands for the building of the dam to be stopped, both in Norway and from far beyond. What's really important to realise is that suddenly the Norwegians were aware of having, and of needing to have, a bad conscience. The whole story of centuries of oppression of the Sami people came out for the first time. The truth is that no one on any side of the debate had a clue just how big all this was to become.

✱ ✱ ✱

But back in Finnmark things were more complicated, both in mainstream Norwegian communities and among the Sami. Not everyone supported these young upstarts in their *lavvo* outside the parliament building, nor did they necessarily agree with the hunger strike. Such a response shouldn't be interpreted as merely cynical; there was genuine concern about what all this was going to do to the Sami cause in general. After all, wasn't there a danger of ordinary people becoming even more hostile than they had been before? Many Sami were deeply worried because they saw themselves as law-abiding Norwegian citizens as well as members of an ethnic Sami population. They felt that all this somehow took away their Norwegian-ness.

At the same time, preparations began for the creation of a far larger police presence at Ground Zero. The first failure was not going to be repeated. What had been learned was that the local police force couldn't do this themselves; significant reinforcements would have to be brought in. Not only that, the police would be bolstered by military reinforcements. The army offered the provision of jeeps, lorries and helicopters. At some point all this must have been discussed at the highest levels, for here preparations were being made for soldiers to face Norwegian citizens. The plan was to bring in 500 police officers; of these, 350 would be from the Oslo area.

And then Prime Minister Odvar Nordli got cold feet. A week of the Oslo hunger strike had passed when, on 15th October, the government met and announced that all building work on the Alta dam would be suspended for the time being. Not only that, but the reindeer herders would be listened to, and there would be a fresh look at the whole project. The hunger strikers were satisfied: to be sure, this was only the end of the beginning, but it was sufficient for them to call off the action. It's now considered they had won something of a victory.

What caused this sudden loss of confidence by the government? In large measure it was due to the young Sami activists and the pitching of their *lavvo* in front of the parliament buildings bang in the middle of Oslo. Large sectors of Norwegian society now believed they were seeing the crushing of a native people, the persecution of an ethnic minority. The government had never anticipated this. From the outset it had been for them about the construction of a necessary dam; it had nothing to do with ethnic conflict. Prime Minister Nordli knew what the building of the dam was now going to mean, namely, the greatest use of manpower imaginable to achieve the completion of the building of a power station. And it wasn't just public opinion at home he had to consider: the international community now knew all about Alta from their newspapers and television screens.

Within the ruling Norwegian Labour Party the cracks could not only be seen they could be heard. There was a very real split over Nordli's sudden order to stop work on the dam: some were enraged at him for what they interpreted as cowardice, while others saw him as nothing less than a brave statesman. One quoted Lenin, saying he had taken a step back in order to take two forward. And all of it was really as a result of the *lavvo* action: the government simply had no idea how to tackle what had become an ethnic conflict.

What they did now was to attempt to put their finger on the pulse of local Sami opinion. They quickly got a sense of the near hatred that existed between the coastal Sami communities and those deep in the heartlands of Finnmark. Some of that was due to ancient cultural differences, but at least a proportion of it could be attributed to generations of forced *fornorsking* (Norwegianisation). Such policies had been particularly successful on the coast. (An illustration of this comes to mind with the much more recent putting up of road signs in Sami: local people themselves in the coastal regions of Arctic Norway lost no time in tearing the signs down).

Nevertheless, the Nordli government set about establishing a three-pronged plan for the tackling of Sami grievances – from land rights to language rights, and everything in between. This plan was made public just before Christmas in 1979. Sami organisations were cautiously pleased, but they weren't going to accept that the Alta question should be split off from everything else. The ruling Labour Party was itself divided now over the building of the dam, but it was nonetheless seen as unlikely that parliament would vote against its construction, having been so strongly in favour in the past. That was proved absolutely correct: on 30th May 1980 the building of the Alta dam was once more strongly endorsed by parliament.

In the wake of this there was a new momentum to get things moving in terms of the construction work: hitherto the wheels had all been grinding terribly slowly. But the protestors remained a force to be reckoned with. There had to be ways found to contain them and even to break down their growing strength. It was fundamentally important that new waves of protestors were prevented from travelling to Alta; there was a resolve to arrest protestors and to detain them for as long as possible, and to prevent others from reaching certain sectors of the site. But how exactly was all this to be achieved?

The whole idea of the deployment of the military was controversial: there was no appetite for direct confrontation between protestors and soldiers – that was out of the question. But there could be military resources and military protection for the police camp, though it was important all this was defined and declared in legal terms.

Behind the scenes there was a huge amount of legal debate as to precisely what could and couldn't be done in respect of the involvement of the military. Finally it was agreed that a naval vessel could sit off the coast of Finnmark to provide lodgings for the 600 police officers. Finally too the highest court in the land delivered its verdict on the whole question of the construction of the dam: by a margin of four votes to three it was declared legal, so although the government was given a yes, it was a weak yes. Nonetheless, they had been waiting long and patiently for this confirmation of their position and now it had been given. They had to act swiftly or risk looking indecisive. D-Day was to be 14th January 1981.

There was almost a stillness as before battle that day. It was the very middle of an Arctic winter: protestors were in *lavvos* and tents, even snow holes. On the other side were members of the special branch: one of their number actually spoke Sami. There had been an attempt to find some kind of last-minute compromise: that was something the prime minister would have given his eye teeth to achieve. There had been a secret meeting between the chief of police and two professors who were part of the protest camp. One thing the chief of police wanted to establish was that the protestors had no weapons: that could be confirmed without doubt. Both sides tried hard to persuade the other to back down. Neither would.

The Sami sat at the front of the protestors: it was a symbolic position as they were the ones who had come first to this land. They were made up not only of Norwegian Sami; others were from Sweden and Finland – about fifty of them in all. Around them, in tents, were the real diehards who had chained themselves together. By this stage of the campaign there was a mood of absolute determination to prevent the construction of the Alta dam. It's reckoned that a good number of the protestors would have been willing to give their lives for the cause had that been necessary. And now was perhaps going to be that point. Nor was it by any means just about the mood there at Ground Zero: across Norway were group after group of local activists, determined that the dam wouldn't become reality. Down in Oslo there was a symbolic protest in front of parliament.

But on the other side of the divide were police officers who were less than enthusiastic about all this. Many had been drafted in from other corners of the country; some were actually quite against the building of the Alta dam themselves. What felt most wrong was that here were ordinary citizens – many of them academics and professionals – legitimately protesting in an utterly law-abiding manner, and facing arrest and possible imprisonment.

What happened next was bizarrely straightforward and completely successful. The police moved in swiftly and efficiently and almost literally carried off the protest camp. Even the diehards in their tents were cut loose and removed: the police had been prepared for every eventuality. By midnight the last of the protestors had been removed and the following day work on the dam began. The entire area was cleared.

For good reason, the activists were hugely demoralised: they had no idea it was all going to be over in the blink of an eye. Had it not been the middle of January a new set of protestors would have been ready to take the places of those who had been removed. The timing of the response by the government was near perfect. But there wasn't much chance for the protestors to do some urgent thinking: before they knew what to do next a camp they had established not far away from Ground Zero was torn down and the activists found there arrested. This was a controversial action: it was felt that the police were becoming tougher, that the swoop on the camp itself had been unlawful. There was a belief too that conversations had been listened to, something that was always strenuously denied.

* * *

But it wasn't all over yet, not by a long way. The next chapter involved a group of ultra-radical Sami, and their first action almost reads as something out of a fantasy novel. One of their number (there were some fourteen or fifteen in an organised network) was Mikkel Eira. He decided to ask King Olav, the Norwegian king, for an audience. The request was granted. Several of the group went to the palace and sat with him and talked for some time. Formalities were all but forgotten: they simply talked. On the one side the Sami spoke about their plight; on the other the king tried to explain what he could and couldn't do. Mikkel Eira said he found the king a most sympathetic man. For one thing he promised he would speak to the politicians about the establishment of a Sami parliament; he said he hoped he might live to see the day it was created. But with tears in his eyes he told them there was nothing he could do about the Alta dam. There was simply no way it could be stopped.

The rest of the Sami group sent a letter to the prime minister, Odvar Nordli, requesting another meeting. They demanded both a halt to the work on the dam and the establishment of a Sami parliament. If these demands couldn't be discussed with the prime minister, there would be drastic consequences.

But Nordli wasn't about to be bullied into submission. He did reply to the delegation, saying he was in contact with "responsible Sami organisations". It was clear he saw this group as too radical. And so Ante Gaup, one of its members, went on hunger strike, and a few days later so did another four from the group. They said that, if necessary, they would die for the cause (the cause really being Alta). But the Sami community in general was sharply divided over this new action; the moderates knew that the government simply was not prepared to deal with activists. There were even some who knew the members on hunger strike and couldn't support what they were doing. But paradoxically enough it was now Odvar Nordli who suddenly fell seriously ill.

It was none other than Gro Harlem Brundtland who took his place. Right away a group of Sami women asked to have a meeting with her. Two days later this took place, but the women – fourteen of them in all – were frustrated that the meeting lasted all of half an hour. So they occupied her office. When word of this reached the hunger strikers, they came to sit in the corridor outside the office. But there was no sign of Brundtland herself. In the end they bedded down for the night on the floor. What's telling is that over the next hours the telephones rang and rang, callers demanding that the women literally be thrown from the building – and many of the callers were from northern Norway. More than anything this illustrates the sharp divide within the northern community.

In the meantime the hunger strikers were whisked off to Sweden because it was feared the Norwegian authorities would start to force-feed them. Mikkel Eira would rather they had wheeled hospital beds right into the parliament building for the media storm it would have created, but the others were not to be persuaded.

Gro Harlem Brundtland was now in a very deep and dangerous quagmire. The pressure on her regarding Alta and the Sami was by no means just domestic; it was very much also international. But she had to put to one side her own views concerning the case: she was the leader of parliament, and parliament had declared time and time again its commitment to this hydro-electric scheme. Many were absolutely determined that for what they perceived as the fundamental basis of democracy there could be and should be no U-turn. At the same time she recognised there had to be give and take, through dialogue, not least because of the more extreme elements within the Sami movement. She wanted to find a reason to stop the work on the Alta dam for the time being, to allow the whole situation to calm and cool. The Sami themselves were involved in a secret meeting in Kautokeino to try to find a solution to her dilemma. What was concocted was, frankly, something that no one had thought of before. It was announced that no exploration of the Finnmark site had been made for Sami remains; that would have to be done before the work went on. In this way the poison was very much taken out of the wound. The hunger strike came to an end and the police presence at Ground Zero was greatly reduced. Once again work came to a standstill. The protestors hoped, of course, that this would be the end of it all.

* * *

The campaign continued, but interest in the whole protest was beginning to wane. Efforts were kept up to find evidence of potential damage to salmon numbers in the Alta River and effects on plant life; there were wild hopes of the discovery of genuine Sami artefacts that would render continuation of the work impossible. But the truth was that now the state was absolutely determined the dam and the hydro-electric plant were going to be built. The Oslo parliament had been given the mandate to carry out the building – not once but several times – and civil disobedience was not going to win the day.

That meant there was a feeling the authorities had lost patience with the protestors. They had been given free rein to make their views known for long enough; work had been stopped time and again. Now the cases of those arrested at Ground Zero were processed and fines handed out; judges were brought into Finnmark to deal with cases more swiftly. Fines were deliberately high to deter others from considering taking part.

It was in October 1981 that work began again, and so did the protesting. Some 400 came to demonstrate their opposition, though tactics now had to change purely and simply because of the hefty nature of the fines: they simply couldn't be afforded indefinitely.

But it wasn't that anger had ebbed away: not in the least. Reindeer herding groups were incensed that this new work at the site had started without any warning. They saw this as a clear breach of promises made to them earlier in the year. The difficulty on the other side was that the authorities wanted to take the protestors by surprise, to give them no warning of the re-commencement of work. But in not communicating their intentions they had broken their word to the Sami. This was the very time of the autumn migration of the reindeer, and the work at the dam was right in the middle of that corridor of movement. As a result, reindeer herding groups wanted to break off all contact with government bodies: this was the last straw.

At the same time protestors were no less opposed to the building of the dam: it had become now a cause much bigger than itself. But the removal of the main camp by the police had taken them totally by surprise and it was clear that there was little sense attempting to repeat their old tactics. Opposition still had to be in the form of non-violent direct action, but it had to be carried out very differently.

A new base camp for the protest was established closer to where the dam was to be built. The land belonged to the Duke of Roxburgh, a passionate salmon fisherman, and a man very much opposed to the hydro-electric scheme. What were employed now were guerrilla-type actions by small groups of individuals. Often these Commando-style operations were conducted under cover of darkness. But these actions by their very nature were dangerous, and the whole protest was beginning to falter in terms of its strategy, its way forward. More and more there was an awareness that the state had made up its mind this dam was going to be built and this project completed, that all necessary resources would be employed to ensure its success.

Some of the veteran protestors were remanded in custody; those who couldn't or wouldn't pay fines were imprisoned. Slowly but surely the blood was being drained from the campaign, and in the end the reluctant decision was made to stop fighting. There were some whispers about sabotage actions, but these were immediately quashed by the activists' central committee. The four main leaders of the protest movement were sentenced to between twenty and ninety days in prison. So that was the end of the campaign.

* * *

No, not quite. There were four Sami who believed that all the way along everything had been too passive. They were determined to make a last statement, to undertake some kind of symbolic action. Together they went to a home guard depot in the Tana region of Finnmark and broke in. They stole some grenades and the intention was to place these on a bridge that led to the site back in Alta. The intention seems to have been to create little more than a firework display, not actually to blow up the bridge. But the truth is that no one knows for sure; it may be that they *thought* that's what they'd do. At any rate a grenade went off at the wrong time and one of the four lost an arm and his sight in one eye; once it was possible he fled the country for the next two years. The police were then convinced there was a Sami guerrilla group operating, though in reality nothing of the kind existed. But there might well have been other such actions if that one hadn't gone so horribly wrong.

EIGHT

After Alta

BUT WHAT DOES THE LANDSCAPE look like now, politically and culturally, all these years after the struggle to save a river that grew into the battle to recognise a people? Certainly the first of those causes was lost; the Alta River was dammed and the hydro-electric scheme constructed. The irony is, though, that even the most hardened protestors will admit the destruction of the river simply didn't happen. It's still an important salmon river (perhaps the fish that are pulled from its magnificent fast-flowing stretches aren't quite as huge as once they were), but salmon there are in plenty all the same.

But what of the struggle it became, a campaign to get the Oslo government and really the whole of Norway to recognise the Sami at last and to acknowledge and honour their rights? At the time of the beginning of the struggle being Sami was barely recognised at all: there were no language rights, no support for reindeer herders, and even the singing of the traditional *joik* was ostensibly not allowed. In legal terms, the Sami simply didn't exist, and they were discriminated against – by the state and by wider society. It wasn't just about laws; it was a case of the little comment at a table in the pub, or the snigger from a group of kids in the playground. It was as old as the hills, but it existed and it mattered. It never went away and it was never dealt with.

The *lavvo* action outside the parliament building in Oslo was of immense significance. The conversation, strange and surreal though it was, between the Sami radicals and the king, must have counted once the dust of Alta settled. The fact too that the Sami in their traditional garments chained themselves to diggers at the Alta site, and journalists from around the world came and asked them for their story – that has to have mattered. It wasn't just that the people of Norway at last discovered who their neighbours were; it was that the rest of the world did too.

The Nordli government had made all sorts of promises to the Sami community during the Alta campaign, and those promises couldn't just be ignored. The fact that young Sami radicals had gone as far as they had was of importance because it showed the Sami were no longer prepared to meekly accept all they were told to do. They had shown finally that they were prepared to flex a muscular arm.

So new recognition was given to the reindeer herders and to the Sami language. In 1989 King Olav opened the Sami parliament in Karasjok; he had personally expressed his desire to see it established not all that long before and now it had become a reality. And, as important as all these rights enshrined in law, was the simple right of people to be who they wanted to be. That was the fundamental right the state (and sometimes church and state had gone hand in glove in their activities) had tried to deny the Sami. It was about trying to take away a language and a very identity.

The Sami won respect through the Alta campaign: a genuine guilt was felt by large sectors of Norwegian society for what they had not really been aware was being done, or had chosen not to open their eyes to see before. There was a desire to do things differently, not just to be concerned at the plight of Amazonian tribes or native peoples in Borneo, but to be aware at last of an ethnic minority in their own midst. And it was about the little things as well as the big: the under-the-breath name-calling in the gym queue and the behind-the-hand comments on the bus. It was about the winning of respect and the giving of respect.

Rome wasn't built in a day and political correctness can itself be a dangerous fig-leaf. But it was a start, a serious start. It says everything that today you'll hear Sami being spoken without a second thought in the centre of Alta or Karasjok by groups of confident youngsters. It counts for a great deal that Norwegians are suddenly proud of the fact they have a Sami cousin, or that their daughter is engaged to a reindeer herder. And they are.

There are Sami programmes on NRK (the main broadcasting corporation in Norway and the equivalent of the BBC both for television and radio output). Important films have been made about Sami stories and from the perspective of the people: significant first and foremost because it demonstrates what Sami artists are capable of. Before Alta the Sami were a hidden minority. If wider society had an impression of them at all (and often they didn't), it might be of work-shy and not-always-sober individuals, of reindeer herders in weird outfits who spoke in sing-song voices, of a people who received too many hand-outs from the state.

Perhaps such preconceptions and prejudices linger, or at least the last tattered rags of them, and especially in the bigger towns of southern Norway. But the glass is half-full rather than half-empty; the Sami have come in from the cold and have won respect in Norway. At best they're valued; their language and culture allowed to live and breathe in serious ways, and they're noticed as never before.

That's Norway, at least. The Alta effect is noted by its absence over the borders in Arctic Sweden and Finland, and into the Kola Peninsula of Arctic Russia. Yes, Sweden and Finland have parliaments for their respective Sami communities, but the evolution in the perception of their culture has happened to nothing like the same degree. It is likely to be worst in Russia, where treatment of the Sami back in the bad old days of the Soviet era was abominable: reindeer were taken from the herders and shot while the people themselves were forced to abandon their traditional way of life and adopt a settled existence in concrete homes. When the Wall came done at last and the Cold War was over, Sami from the Western side went at once to see what remained of their cultural brothers and sisters. They found precious little.

But the picture in Norway is complicated too. After Alta the reindeer herders were recognised: it was as if the government in Oslo suddenly said, "Ah, we know who you people are! You're the ones with the reindeer and you want recognition! Will this do?" Money was thrown at the "problem" in the hope that it might make a difference or even go away. It might well be deemed to have been well-intentioned, but while it perhaps helped to ease part of the problem, it caused others.

Because the Sami are by no means all reindeer herders. Others are farmers; plenty are fishermen living along the northern coasts. In short, the Sami aren't one thing: they are many. It's true that the iconic image of the Arctic Sami is of a reindeer herder from Finnmark, but by rewarding one part of the whole community the Oslo government was inadvertently neglecting the rest. That inevitably led to a large number feeling forgotten, and it caused resentment. There were already schisms between the inland herders in Finnmark and the fishermen on the coast; this now helped add fuel to the fire, not dampen the flames. It's true that nowadays the reindeer herding community is seen as doing very well: families may have a winter house in Karasjok or Kautokeino, and they may have a place up on the northern coast for when they're there during the summer months.

The greatest number of Gaelic speakers in Scotland live in Glasgow: by far and away the largest number of Norwegian Sami live in Oslo and satellite towns. Often they have married outwith the community to live "settled" lives, they are carpenters and bus drivers and teachers and anything you care to consider. But it might well be true to say that they know as little about operating a reindeer as they do about operating a tractor. They have become townies.

I think back to that unforgettable four-hour talk with my first Sami friend, Lars Johnsen. His father had been a Sami, his mother a settled, southern Norwegian. Lars had grown up with a foot in both worlds, though he didn't fully appreciate his schizophrenic relationship with himself until he went to live in Finnmark for the first time. Who was he? What was he? He had grown up in an eastern Norwegian town, and on the outside he was a football-loving boy from the south. But his father had come from Tana, and that landscape and its river and its salmon – its very blood – was embedded within him. And when he went back there he felt the drumbeat of it and the call of it; he saw his people all around him but he couldn't speak their language and he couldn't truly call himself one of them. He was looking in the window of a house that somehow belonged to him. Yet he didn't have the key to its door, or if he did then he had to learn how to open it.

It's little different for a Sami youngster who goes south. Gone are the days when the use of the Sami language would be punished at school; gone too are the days when Sami pupils are made to feel their cultural identity must be seen as inferior and exorcised and left behind. No, all pupils are equal; any bright child, Sami or Norwegian (or other), has the same chance and the same right to reach university and of emerging to become a lawyer or a doctor or whatever else. So let's say that the Sami pupil becomes a student and goes from Finnmark to study in Trondheim or Bergen or Oslo; they work hard for a year perhaps and all goes well. And then one morning they wake up and, quite literally, wonder who they are. They're training to be something high-powered in the settled world and they remember that their grandfather, or even their father, was a reindeer herder. Who are they and what are they becoming? What *have* they become? What have they allowed themselves to become?

And at worst it can lead back to that graveyard in Karasjok where Lars took me all those years ago, to the resting places of young Sami – boys, especially – who couldn't

cope with the schizophrenia any more. They didn't know
who they were or what direction in which to go, and they
took their own lives.

My feeling is that, politically, the Sami have never been
stronger but that, culturally, everything is oddly fragile.
What does it *mean* to be Sami today? It seems that it's
sufficient simply to *feel* Sami, for there's a fear that defining identity through language or occupation will create
barriers. A Sami political activist on television will often
come across as almost deliberately non-stereotypically
Sami. While one can understand that because of centuries
of struggle (and discrimination), if the stereotype is what's
being escaped from, one sometimes wonders precisely
what's left.

Life in the northernmost part of Norway, in Finnmark,
becomes no easier. Since the high days of the Alta dam
campaign, the problems have changed. I made mention
of those other Sami, the fishermen and farmers and crafts
people, who feel every bit as much Sami but who don't
happen to herd reindeer. And they're not the only ones
to feel resentment; it's also ordinary Norwegians who're
trying to eke out a living from an unforgiving north. They
will roll their eyes and say they weren't blessed by being
born under a Sami star; they feel like second-class citizens
because their reindeer-herding neighbours got all the ben-
efits and all the recognition. And that in turn points back
to some of the age-old divides at the heart of Finnmark,
deep divides.

And to whom does all this wild country belong? The
same question that was being asked at the height of the
struggle over Alta is no less important today. The difference

is that now it's mining companies that want to move in to exploit mineral resources under the tundra. At the time of Alta the tundra was seen as next to useless; now it is known to be concealing gold and diamonds and much more. Thus far the state has not given permission for mining, but one wonders for how long that can last.

When I visited Karasjok for the writing of this book, I spoke to local Sami about these threats. They had no more faith in the state than back in the days of the battle for Alta; if it was politically expedient for the state to open up tracts of land to the diggers, it would happen. Suspicion and fear seem as strong as ever, and they may be justified. But one likes to believe, to hope, that something has changed once and for all. The Sami thought they were saving a river and something of themselves when they joined the struggle for Alta. On paper they lost and the dam was built. But they didn't; they won and they have gone on winning for all these years. The parliament in Karasjok is testament to that. Something incredible was born after Alta, and it's still alive and well and strong. It's not about to disappear.

NINE

Beneath the Ice

THE FIRST TIME I SAW GREENLAND I cried. I had dreamed of being here, and now at last I was seeing it from the open sea – a child's fantasy kingdom of unimaginably sharp peaks reaching into the sky. And around us innumerable white islands; strange shapes of ice, some of them taller than the ship whose deck I stood on. Hours later we came closer, in to our first port of call, and there was a tiny cluster of yellow, red and blue wooden houses, as many dogs as people, and a whole flock of beautiful children who came running down to greet us as the first of us came ashore. That is set to be one of the greatest days of my life, and Greenland is likely to remain for me the most magnificent country I have ever seen. But nonetheless I know that what I did was wrong. The cruise culture, and all it brings with it, is simply the last thing Greenland needs; in fact, I believe it will play a part in destroying this fragile and precious place.

To understand why, I think it's necessary to have a sense of where Greenland has come from. Before telling that story, it's worth explaining why I was on the cruise ship to begin with. What had taken me there was my long-held passion for northern-ness: northern places and peoples. After university I had spent that year in Arctic Norway because I wanted to find the Sami, the reindeer herders whose lands had been poisoned by Chernobyl. But my near obsession with the Sami story led me on to explore other northern indigenous groups and their struggles for recognition and political rights: chief among them, the Greenlandic Inuit. Now I was there for the first time, delivering a lecture on Inuit culture.

Greenland is a Danish colony, and although the Danes were very aware of not wanting to impose their culture on an indigenous Arctic people that already had their own, what exists now is a strange confusion. At the centre of the old Inuit existence was hunting, and for many of the southern Greenlandic communities, hunting has all but disappeared. The burden of this loss has fallen particularly heavily on men: their self-worth and pride have been lost. More than that, they don't have enough to do and are condemned to live settled lives that have no purpose. A dangerous mix of frustration and redundancy is the result, and this is far too often taken out on women and children with tragic consequences. Greenland's tiny population includes a heart-breaking number of children in care.

Whose fault is all this? Apportioning blame now is well-nigh impossible and ultimately futile. It is partly the result of the law of unintended consequences: the fact is that the Danes set out to control Greenland in a way that would impinge on and interfere with native life as little as possible. Their planning was enlightened and mature, but deciding everything on paper was never going to be the same as carrying it out on the ground. Very little could prepare any

Dane for the severity of a Greenlandic winter. There had to be dealings between the two communities, but culturally they were so remote from each other – to the extent that one often has the sense of two men standing on respective cliff-tops, trying to shout across. All that each can hear is noise; not a single actual word is audible.

But the result is nonetheless that many Greenlanders blame the Danes. They have had Home Rule for decades now, but they clamour for full independence. Oil, mining, cruise tourism: one has a sense at times of the Greenlanders seeking to throw themselves into the arms of anyone with a wallet who can take them away from their old colonial lords and masters. One of my abiding memories is of leaving that cruise ship and walking down a wrong street in Qaqortoq away from our guide. I found myself standing staring at a boy wearing a sweatshirt bearing the logo of one of our internationally recognised oil companies. That seemed to say it all.

Denmark still supports Greenland to the hilt. Vast amounts of resources are flown in from Copenhagen to fill the supermarkets of the capital, Nuuk, with all the goodies that the rest of Western Europe demands. Greenland may weigh heavily now on the conscience of Denmark, but she must also weigh heavily on her purse-strings.

Nuuk is one of the saddest places I have visited in all my life. The arrival from the sea was utterly breathtaking. The snow-capped fairy tales of Greenland's mountains lay behind; beautiful fjord arms stretching north and south, and out on a blue sea the strange sculptings of icebergs. Yet as we came closer, Nuuk began to take shape, and what dominated were rows and rows of slums. Grey desolations of buildings that might be expected in the poorest suburbs of an Eastern European city, home to thousands of Greenlandic Inuit who barely know their own identify any more. I walked through the streets of Nuuk early in the morning and it wasn't long before I saw men and women heading home with bags full of chinking bottles.

It would be wrong and dangerous to imply that this is the whole story of Nuuk or indeed of Greenland. But it's the sadness that one sees that lingers, the sadness of a people who are in the wrong homes and living the wrong lives, and who do not know what to do to escape from either. This is a priceless culture that's survived everything 10,000 winters have thrown at it. I feel as strongly about the struggle for survival of the Greenlandic Inuit as I do about that of the polar bear. They are part of the same delicate web of ice.

Yet, as I have said, Greenland is not all Nuuk. This country's population is also strung out, mainly along the west coast, in tiny communities of huddled, brightly-coloured wooden houses. There's plenty of pride too, in fishing a still plentiful sea, and in farming. Age-old craft skills survive: women and men carve and sew. This was a shamanic world, and that's reflected in the extraordinary masks and paintings still created by Inuit artists. That ancient culture has been buried, but it is not dead: it exists below the surface – one might almost say beneath the ice.

It's for that reason I believe so passionately that a cruise culture is as wrong for Greenland every bit as much as uranium mines and the drilling for oil. What remains of Greenlandic culture is thin and fragile: the last thing it needs is more disturbance. Greenlanders might see cruise tourism as another answer in the fight against Danish dependency, but it feels almost like the choosing of prostitution by a girl desperate to get away from her parents.

Imagine one of the larger cruise ships landing at Nanortalik, Narsaq or Qaqortoq, one of these smaller communities on the south-west coast of Greenland. Thousands of people swarm out among a scattering of houses that support a community of 500: those tourists want to speak English, they want to find souvenirs and they want Internet access. Think about the effect on that tiny community in just one single day: the whole of their ordinary way of life is interrupted, altered – perhaps changed in certain ways forever. The tail is in danger of wagging the dog: changes being made to ways of living in order to bring in more revenue – at any price.

Cruise companies may make nice noises about caring for and supporting the places they visit in this region, but I remain deeply sceptical. At worst it becomes a kind of raping and pillaging, before the ship is off to the next port of call. Cruise passengers want the equivalent of tasty morsels; bite-size pieces of cultural experience they can chew and spit out before going on to taste the next. On my voyage it seemed to be summed up for me in one act: some of the Filipino crew on my ship took one of the dinghies out to an iceberg lying close to the stern. Passengers stood on the deck excited and clicking their cameras as the boys cut off chunks of 10,000-year-old ice – that were then brought back for our drinks later that evening.

Some of the first ships to visit Greenland were from the ports of Scotland. They were whaling vessels, and eventually the Greenlandic communities took to fleeing up into the hills when they saw the white sails and great masts on the horizon. At one time they did the same on the Hebridean island of St Kilda, for the population feared that ships were bringing sickness with them. And that is why the Greenlanders fled, because far too frequently the Scottish sailors carried sexually transmitted diseases the native people came to know and fear all too well. It's worth mentioning that one of the factors in the death of St Kilda was the impact of early cruise ships.

This is a new age and yet somehow I almost wish the Greenlanders might run again into the hills when they see the tell-tale smoke of cruise vessels that come bearing an illness, an illness that has no name. Yet it is composed of a Western malaise that is made up of too-muchness, of over-indulgence. We come from a culture that has never had so much and yet never felt so empty. As it is rightly said, we know the price of everything and the value of nothing.

Yet the paradox is that it's our Western living which so many in the developing world yearn to emulate and espouse. Greenland is in many ways part of that developing world, right on the northern edge of Europe. Perhaps it is inevitable that the old Greenland will be swamped in the end by that Western world, but it surely doesn't mean we have to accelerate the process.

Greenland has been blessed with a haunting plenitude of natural wonders. Yet it is very much suffering the first ravages of climate change. I remember talking to one elderly man on that south-west coast; he told me that in his childhood the sea froze so solid year on year that they used to drive out on the ice to visit each other. Now, he told me, the ice retreats ten miles each year: there is no sea ice whatsoever today on that water in front of his window.

Yet there is good reason for hope. Greenland is the biggest island in the world; it is a vast natural kingdom that we still can choose to look after responsibly. Eco-tourism could be managed in such a way that it brings much-needed revenue to the country without destroying the very majesty people yearn to experience.

An eco-tourism that could benefit the Inuit population to the hilt, employing local men in particular to lead expeditions and teach traditional skills so that pride in the old ways can be restored. Greenland's infrastructure is not equipped for the sudden arrival of thousands of tourists: it's much better suited to coping with small groups of adventurers coming to experience the mountains, the fjords, the botany. Better by far such small groups than shiploads of cruise passengers.

Not least because Greenland has no roads. It is extraordinary and wonderful to visit a country of such vastness and see no traffic, experience no dual carriageways. As a writer I think of roads sometimes both in real terms and as metaphor. A few years back, when Latvia was liberating herself from the old Soviet Union, I wrote a poem for my friend Ivars from Riga.

It was about holding onto the hope of a new future; seeing the promise of a different way ahead. But the lines could have been written for Greenland too as she stands on the threshold of a new beginning, believing there are other ways to choose than the tired, false roads of Western capitalism. There are better things than cruise ships; better answers than the mining of uranium.

If a man should come now to your door selling motorways
A rustle of money in his eyes;
Do not buy his road, for it leads
To all our lost riches, our need of God.

TEN

Taking up the Pen

IT CAN'T HAVE HELPED the Sami cause in earlier centuries when the settlers realised that they neither wrote books nor read them. Their culture was an oral one; the Sami had a mythological world every bit as strong as the Norse one, and stories were passed down – as they always are – from mother to daughter and father to son. There are central figures in these tales that appear again and again; just as in the Inuit story world, there's often a great deal of mutilation and cruelty. But then the real stories that were collected from our forests and our valleys – the ones that weren't sanitised and published in attractive anthologies – feature just as much brutality.

I have a copy of the first book written in the Sami language by a Sami. It appeared in 1910 from a reindeer herder by the name of Johan Turi. He had been encouraged to compile the work by an artist and ethnologist called Emilie Demant. *Turi's Book of Lappland* is a most candid and straightforward account of the world he knew. One wonders how others around him in the Sami community viewed this frankness at the height of the worst time of forced assimilation, when being Sami was well-nigh a crime. The book is particularly revealing about Sami beliefs and customs.

Two years later, the first novel appeared in the Sami language. *Daybreak* was presented as fiction, but written by Anders Larsen to make abundantly clear the struggle it was to be Sami at that time, and pointing the way forward to the hope of a brighter future. Another writer from his generation was Matti Aikio; he was very much a Sami but he chose to write in Norwegian. Unlike Anders Larsen he believed that the struggle was effectively over already; the Sami were so racially intermixed, he believed, that their culture was gone or close to vanishing. Perhaps the fact that Aikio chose to live in Oslo and use Norwegian as his first language says it all. His love of his people and culture still shines through in his writing, just the same, even if he did think it was all too late.

In 1940 came a collection of poems and short stories by the Finnish Sami writer Hans Aslak Guttorm. Then, after something of a silence, there came a veritable flourishing of creative activity in the 1970s, and I find this important and exciting because it ties in completely with the period of the rise of the great Gaelic writers in Highland Scotland. Politically it's a time of renewed struggle for the respective languages and cultures, but in so many ways it also feels like it should be a death rattle: not so much the phoenix rising from the ashes as the phoenix giving a final beautiful cry before being engulfed in the flames forever. What's interesting is that it was a time of flourishing for native cultures in many other corners of the globe.

Yet real recovery was coming just the same, to both the Sami and the Highland worlds. The first Sami publishing company came into being at the end of the 1970s. But there were the same problems as the Gaels across the water faced. There were many who had never been educated in Sami; many others had "lost" their native language as a result of the *fornorsking* process. This meant that the only hope of accessing Sami literature would be through translations, but providing these for relatively miniscule numbers of people was well-nigh impossible without government subsidy.

Here Norway has been enormously generous to its writers and publishers alike. For long enough something has existed called *innkjøpsordningen* – not a term you'd be expected to remember at the breakfast table. What it means, in essence, is that when a new book is published anywhere in Norway, 1,000 copies are immediately bought up by the government. What *that* means is that every library from Stavanger to Kirkenes – and everywhere in between along the country's bony spine – will obtain a copy of the book. The fact is that most of these works will end up deep in the basement never to be seen again, but of course it is a very practical way of supporting authors. Poetry in particular has almost no market at all in Norway. I remember working with a group of Norwegian poets at the Edinburgh International Book Festival; they were all relatively well known at home, but they admitted quite frankly that new volumes of their work would sell somewhere in the region of forty to fifty copies. Without *innkjøpsordningen* it would be impossible to make even a semblance of a living. Of course there has to be more support than this, especially for those trying to exist from something as fragile as poetry, but it's an important component in the struggle nonetheless.

Just as it is for Sami authors whose reading communities – whether in the host language or in translation – are infinitesimally small. Yet I have found lovely hardback copies of the work of Sami writers well displayed in bookshops hundreds of miles south of the main Sami heartland.

The flowering of Sami writing in Norway has come first and foremost from women. It's as if they were the ones who got up, metaphorically speaking, to pull their culture and their language out of the ditch into which both had fallen. It's as if the men sat and hung their heads in despair. Inevitably it's a rather dangerously simplistic picture I paint, but it's women writers who've certainly been the primary force over the most recent decades. There was Kirsti Paltto to begin with – the most versatile and prolific of them all. There's Rauni Magga Lukkari, also born in the 1940s, but very much a poet only. Then there's Synnøve Persen, who is known first and foremost as a visual artist, though in her work words and paintings collide and meld. Ellen Marie Vars writes for young people, as does Inger Haldis Halvari.

Having said all that, Nils Aslak Valkeapää stands head and shoulders clear of them all: female and male alike. Tragically he was involved in a serious car accident and died in 2001, far too soon, at the very height of his prowess. I have offered a translation from one of his poems at the beginning of this book; I have written too about his most haunting *joik*. Somehow he embodies the whole being of the Sami as a musician, poet and painter. It is worth seeking out his beautiful *The Sun, My Father* from 1991, for which he was awarded the Nordic Prize for Literature. It's worth finding *Trekways of the Wind* too. Perhaps more than any other Sami author he gets to the heart of what it means to be part of this land, to have it buried deep within the soul. It can't begin to be understood by those for whom the land is something to be bought and sold, owned and possessed.

With the click of a mouse these days you can have the magnificent and haunting voice of Nils Aslak Valkeapää in your home. Once upon a time, back when I was visiting him that first time in Karasjok, my friend Lars pressed a cassette recording of Nils Aslak's *joiks* into my hand. It was difficult for Lars to do so because he came from a Laestadian church tradition where *joik* is still awkwardly tolerated (if at all). I'm only grateful that he did.

ELEVEN

Finding the Way Back

I STAYED CLOSE TO ALTA for the writing of this book, for fairly obvious reasons. I arrived in the middle of winter, having travelled north by all modes of transport possible except plane. That would have felt wrong, arriving too easy.

Train to Oslo from Bergen, and then the night train to Trondheim. I had forgotten that I was older, a lot older than when I first came to live in Norway, and the night train was as uncomfortable as it always had been, my back at a purgatorial angle in the reclining metal seat. Then onto the train to Bodø at eight o'clock in the morning, and all the memories came rushing back. The excitement of knowing I was going north, north of the Arctic Circle. The scents of fresh rolls and tobacco; soldiers and young people and girlfriends, their last pieces of conversation before the rust-red doors were slammed and the train started out of the station. I felt no different despite the years that had disappeared. I was going back for a month to the Arctic world where I had lived a whole year. I was going back to write the Sami story that had first set me alight in 1991.

It wasn't really winter in Trondheim, not what I had hoped for. But it became winter on the eight-hour journey north, bit by bit. When I got off the train in Fauske the snow was deep and more of it falling. My shoes made the *knirking* sound the Sami smile at, for their shoes – their original ones – made no sound at all in the snow. They can hear the rest of us coming, because of the *knirking* of our shoes.

I stayed overnight in a cabin outside Fauske, two stations short of Bodø, the end of the line. It's where Norway's at its very narrowest; on good, clear days you have the sea on one side and Sweden on the other. Now it just snowed and the silence closed in; it was the beginning of the year and no one else was staying in any of the cabins. I listened to news of road closures and avalanches, wondered if I'd get to Bodø at all the following day. But I slept like a felled tree, still exhausted after my near-sleepless night on the Trondheim train.

I got to Bodø all right the next morning, and waited in a tiny shelter by the edge of the fjord for the vessel that was to take me to Tromsø. All the weather in the world seemed to be coming in that morning; little at all was visible beyond the windows.

I never made it to dinner on board that night; the ship was tossed on ferocious seas as my belongings clattered about the cabin. The following day it was better, but still winter. It was as though I had travelled north of all colour; for hours we passed jagged cliffs and islets that were nothing but grey. And then all at once we would call in at some tiny port and past the whirling snowflakes were yapping dogs and cars and a few brave lights.

A group of northern Norwegians would come onboard, living up to their bright-eyed and cheerful reputation. It's said of a northern Norwegian that if they see someone standing outside their house vomiting, having just come ashore, they'll call out, "Don't stand there and be sick! Come in and be sick!"

We arrived in Tromsø in the early afternoon and I had two hours to wait for the bus. I wished I had time to go to the edge of town and the university, to visit my friend the Sami Professor of Literature, Harald Gaski. It would have been good to knock on his door unannounced after many years of silence. But there was time only for a snatched meal and the finding of the right bus stop. Then it was the start of a six-hour journey to Alta. At times it was akin to being on the back of a horse; the bus plunged into descents and tore along the edges of mountainsides. I was amazed at just how many were on that bus: they got off at the remotest corners and disappeared into darkness. There's little in the way of talk; you don't thank your driver or even offer a smile. It all just happens and there are no delays or cancellations.

And in the end, at last, I reached Alta. And someone was there to meet me and called out my name in the darkness. And it felt like the best thing in the world.

✳ ✳ ✳

I fell on the ice that first morning at the Folk High School outside Alta. Everywhere was thick ice, the thickest I have ever encountered. My boarding house was situated beside kennels for huskies; whenever anyone approached the wire fences their heads lifted and they howled. There was no choice but to wear climbing boots every time I went outside; I got my winter legs after that first fall, but there was often a good deal of slithering about on ice hidden by yet another fall of snow.

Every day that I could I took the school bus into Alta and went to the library to study. Here was the special Sami collection I had dreamed there might be: books about *joik*, books about shamanism, books about rock carvings, books about the history of persecution. And there was one book in particular about the story of Alta and the building of the dam; a book that told that story step by careful step.

I spoke to very few people back at the Folk High School. They were students and there at Alta to ski, to climb, to explore. I realised that none of them would even have been born when the Alta campaign was fought; I realised that few of them would have any idea what it meant.

But there was a scattering of other souls, like me, staying at the college. One of them was a young priest by the name of Henrik, and he and I had plenty conversations about Norway's relationships with the Sami, the church's treatment of the Sami, and the Alta case itself then and now. Henrik asked me one day if I had been up to the place where it had all happened, to the site of the protest camp at Stilla. When I replied that I hadn't, he all but drove me then and there that evening. But there was little point going in the dark, and we went instead a day or so later. It brought home to me just how remote a place it was; the car wound up and up the valley, beyond any hope of trees. And all of a sudden we were there; no more than a cattle grid and a sign that had nothing to do with the story of the protest.

I got out of the car and stood there in the cold, and I thought of the pictures I still remembered from my childhood. There was not a single thing here that remembered the story, the greatest chapter of civil unrest in modern Norway – the grassroots campaign that had grown beyond anyone's wildest dreams and all but brought down a government. Not so much as a plaque or a Sami flag, only the sign making clear that driving beyond that spot was for authorised vehicles only. Blue sky and snow, and the hillsides stretching away into silence. I stood there and felt moved just the same, perhaps as much because of the absence of a memorial as by the fact I was standing there in that place at last.

✳ ✳ ✳

Then, however many days later, Kristina Hayward arrived for photographs and for Easter. We were going to stay with Lars and his wife, Biret, in Karasjok, and Easter is a big time for the Sami. A festival close to Kautokeino celebrates the gathering together of the reindeer herds at the end of the long winter; it's a time of competitions and celebration – there are stories to be remembered and shared, old friends to meet again. It's an important time in the Sami church too; it's the season of confirmations, but first and foremost of Easter, that high point in the Christian calendar. Kristina and I wanted to experience as much of all this as we could over the next days.

We drove from Alta, out beyond the Folk High School and south. It was a day of strange light and eerie cloud formations. But the road itself was dry and snowless, despite the still deep drifts around us. For whatever reason we didn't stop at Masi, where the whole story of the Alta dam might have started. This was the Sami community that was almost moved – lock, stock and barrel – and the whole settlement flooded.

Instead we stopped in what I like to call the middle of everywhere for a rest and coffee. Thinking back on the journey now, it was the only café we passed before approaching Karasjok many hours later. There was little here but a house and one or two outbuildings, a track behind that disappeared into snow. We took our lives in our hands getting to the entrance, the ice thick underfoot. But we stepped into a Sami world: paintings on the walls, ornaments, furnishings. For whatever reason it made me think of old Highland farmhouses I had known in childhood, vanished now in a more sophisticated age. But there was nothing pretend about this; it was the real thing. Ironically enough, the café was run by a young Ukrainian. He talked to us about the berries he gathered in autumn to make fruit juice; the way they lived as close to the land as they could. When we left, a girl was talking in Sami on the telephone, young and bright and easy – not a shred of embarrassment about her language and her culture. I couldn't help thinking of my Highland world again; the reluctance to be caught talking Gaelic. After just as much repression, here was a language that was alive and thriving.

We drove on and came to a crossroads: the road went off right to Kautokeino and left to Karasjok. All the time in my head I was hearing a *joik* by Nils Aslak Valkeapää; one of the most haunting songs I have ever known. It lasts a full half-hour and is made up of sounds that repeat, again and again and again, until one is mesmerised by them and quite swept away. I have listened to that *joik* in a darkened room and felt transported by it, carried to another world. And it conjures completely a landscape that is open and endless and huge; a landscape that is somehow beyond words.

Suddenly we started seeing reindeer, little groups of them. They crossed the road, from whiteness into whiteness. Kristina wanted to take pictures, but stopping by the road was difficult because of the sheer depth of the snow. Not long later, suddenly, we came to a lake, and I cried out with the shock of what I was seeing. There were unthinkable numbers of reindeer all across the white rim of the lake. Doubtless it had frozen and snow had fallen on the ice. Now the beasts were there, trying to slake their thirst. They were all down on their front hooves, pawing at the snow-covered ice. We saw it for a matter of seconds and were quite overwhelmed by the wonder of it. But we couldn't stop; there was no chance of stopping. Truly the best pictures are the ones that are never taken.

* * *

The services were long at the Karasjok church, but it felt a privilege to be there just the same. Almost every soul in the congregation was Sami, clad in traditional costume. I could recognise some of the clans; particular hats and designs of costume gave them away. Services were held in Norwegian and Sami: a paragraph of the former first, then the latter. Something new would be explained and then the translation followed. Kristina was wary of taking pictures outside the church: it felt intrusive and unfair. And asking people would have risked formalising the whole process ridiculously.

One afternoon we went to an exhibition of Sami craftwork, a strange assemblage of paintings and books and clothing. Some Sami youngsters arrived; there was no doubting the pride they had in their world, but it was clear they were out to make their costumes modern and stylish just the same. They succeeded, and once more a real self-confidence came across that took me by surprise, that I hadn't expected.

I will admit that I have encountered sad souls in Karasjok in the past; Sami, particularly young men, who have let drink get the better of them and who have nothing better to do than hang around the edges of cafés. Karasjok is very much a Sami community; it has the reputation of being a place of problems, yet that's not easily seen. It may be that the real dark shadows are to be found behind closed doors. But perhaps too the presence of the Norwegian Sami parliament has made a difference to Karasjok in the years since its arrival.

Something else happened while we were there for those days in the town: Lars celebrated his 50th birthday. We had timed things perfectly: we would be there for the celebration, and Kristina was asked if she would take photographs on the day. Biret stayed up all night making cakes and preparing the meal, ensuring the house was ready.

It felt an immense privilege to be present that day. Almost everyone there was Sami, and all in their costumes. John Cesar, Lars and Biret's son, gave a moving speech to his father they hugged for a long time whilst everyone clapped. I found myself in discussion about the Alta dam, about the intervening years, about new threats to the Sami world, about whether people felt stronger than once they had. And I kept thinking of how long this had taken me too, of the journey of years from that first meeting with Lars and the four-hour talk we had had. How little I had known then and how hungry for knowledge I had been. Now, at last, I had something to share; the excitement of a story that is not finished yet, that is still unfolding. I had been set alight by it as a child and now as a middle-aged man I was gathering all the fragments into the semblance of a whole. Perhaps that journey wasn't even done, but this felt a point at which to look out over the land, be glad and grateful. To have been allowed to stand on the edge of this world, to have been welcomed and admitted for a time: what price can be put on that?

Postscript

WHEN I RETURNED TO Highland Perthshire after my year in the Arctic in the early 1990s, I felt quite bereft. Of course that had to do with the friends I had found; the intensity of the Folk High School experience – living in a tight community with sixty or seventy souls for a whole year – means a sudden and total absence of those friends once the experience is over. Many students suffer something akin to bereavement: while I was working on this book in Alta and writing at the Folk High School, I met two former students from the south of Norway who were still staying on the campus. They haven't moved on, literally and metaphorically speaking, because they couldn't bring themselves to leave.

But that's not quite what I mean. The Arctic gets under your skin, into your being. I still remember the nights in midwinter when it was thirty below and I went into the local village to visit friends. There wasn't a sound: it was that snow and ice silence which almost seems bigger than silence itself. The scent of burning pine logs and the blue shadows of the woods on every side. A sky so brim-full of stars it was like the smoke of breath, and the stars crackling diamond-sharp. And I would be back at the college for ten o'clock because that was when the Northern Lights would rise. You never knew what the colours would be, but most often it was the opalescence of blues and greens. I used to think that when they appeared in those first moments they were like the ghosts of horses, rearing up high and falling away once more. Yes, it was the Arctic night I missed more than anything.

But that's not true either. I remember a trip in early autumn we made from the college, though where exactly we went I can't remember. I stayed in a Sami *lavvo*, a wigwam, with two of the Lule Sami students. This was back when I was as excited as a puppy about the whole Sami world, when I must have driven them half-mad with my questions. But that's when we found cloudberries.

The bit of ground where we camped was quite high up; I seem to remember a few stunted birches and pines close by, but nothing more than that. Further away, the moorland stretched to the distance under those rounded, northern hills. It was uncannily like Strathspey, the Cairngorm heartland just north of where I had grown up.

But there in the marshy ground out beyond the trees were tiny, bright dots of orange-gold. We went there later, all of us, to pick sufficient for our sweet that evening. Berries I had never seen before: beaded like raspberries or what I call brambles, except that the beads were a little bigger. I don't know what I expected when I tasted the first one, certainly not this honeyed burst of sweetness lovelier than that of any berry I had known before.

Cloudberries. The Arctic berry so loved by the Sami, and by Sami men in particular. It's almost their designated task to pick them and bring them back. Sometimes in Finnmark those cloudberry-picking trips can last three or four days; they'll stay in a cabin out on the *vidda* (the moorland) and pick during all the long hours of daylight. It's a case of moving from patch to patch. You finish the picking of one area and look up and around, and all at once you catch sight of somewhere new, dotted with spots of orange. That's when they're at their very best, having turned from hard blood-red marbles to soft fruits that have nothing left to do but melt in the mouth.

Yes, if there was one thing I truly missed from that year in the Arctic it was the sheer thrill of walking over the moorland, surrounded only by the sounds of birds, searching for cloudberries. But the year ended just the same; I came back to Perthshire, and slowly but surely the missing began to diminish. And in the end I became a writer.

I don't know how much later it would have been that I was walking on one of our Perthshire hills with family. It was late summer, probably about the middle of August. I stood stock-still because there in front of me, without a shadow of a doubt, was a cloudberry. The berry had long since shrivelled, but that didn't matter. It was the fact it was here, that I hadn't known before!

The following late summer I went to find them on that same hill. And there they were all right, enough to fill a small pail. But it was more than just the finding of them, more than the eating of them afterwards. It was the fact they were there, these berries that took me back to the far north of Norway, and to the Sami.

Every year since then I have gone to that hill to find them in the first or second week of August, depending on how bright and hot the preceding weeks of summer have been. Kristina has been with me, both for the pilgrimage and to capture the journey and the place with photographs. For me it is one of the high points of the year.

But there's something more that I didn't know about until recently. Once upon a time there were shielings all over the Scottish hills. Ironically enough, it's likely the Norse settlers brought the concept of the shieling to Scotland – summer shelters in the hills for the women and children in particular. Yes, there would be plenty of hard work done, but they were places of holiday too, for laughter and play. And they knew all about cloudberries. There is a Gaelic word for cloudberry – *oireag* – and the women and children knew the places where they grew: high up on the hillsides, as much as 2,000ft above the glens. They knew and loved them every bit as much as the Sami men.

So when I go back each late summer for cloudberries I remember all that. And two worlds flow together and grow strangely one, for a little time at least.

Acknowledgements

I have made clear in the pages of the book that this work simply wouldn't have come into being without the existence of the special collection of Sami-related books in Alta library. I want to express again my thanks to library staff for their advice and patience in seeking out material connected to the story of the Alta dam, in particular. I must also offer warm thanks to Alta Folk High School for my accommodation over the weeks of my writing, and as encouragers of the work. And I want to thank Kristina Hayward, not only for the cover image and the photographs at the heart of this book, which are so valuable in bringing the whole Sami story to life, but also for her assistance with research and in reading and preparing the manuscript.

Finally, none of this would have been possible without generous funding from Creative Scotland, nor would the book have seen the light of day without the commitment and support of the team at Saraband. My sincere thanks.

Every effort has been made to trace the copyright holders of the original Sami version of the Nils-Aslak Valkeapää *joik* on pages 15 and 16. The author would be grateful if the copyright holders could contact him about any acknowledgements or corrections that should be incorporated in future editions of this book.

Kenneth Steven has been a full-time writer for more than twenty years. His books have appeared in many languages. www.kennethsteven.co.uk

Kristina Hayward was born and grew up in Sweden. She took up photography after moving to Scotland and has a particular interest in landscape images.